SOVIET PSYCHOLOGY

SOVIET PSYCHOLOGY

A Symposium

With a Foreword by
Ralph B. Winn

GREENWOOD PRESS, PUBLISHERS
WESTPORT, CONNECTICUT

The Library of Congress has catalogued this publication as follows:

Library of Congress Cataloging in Publication Data
Main entry under title:

Soviet psychology.

    Translation of Beiträge aus der Sowjetpsychologie.
    Reprint of the 1961 ed.
    1. Psychology--History--Russia. 2. Psychology--
Addresses, essays, lectures.
[BF108.R8B43 1973]   150'.947   72-9608
ISBN 0-8371-6592-X

CONTENTS

SOVIET PSYCHOLOGY

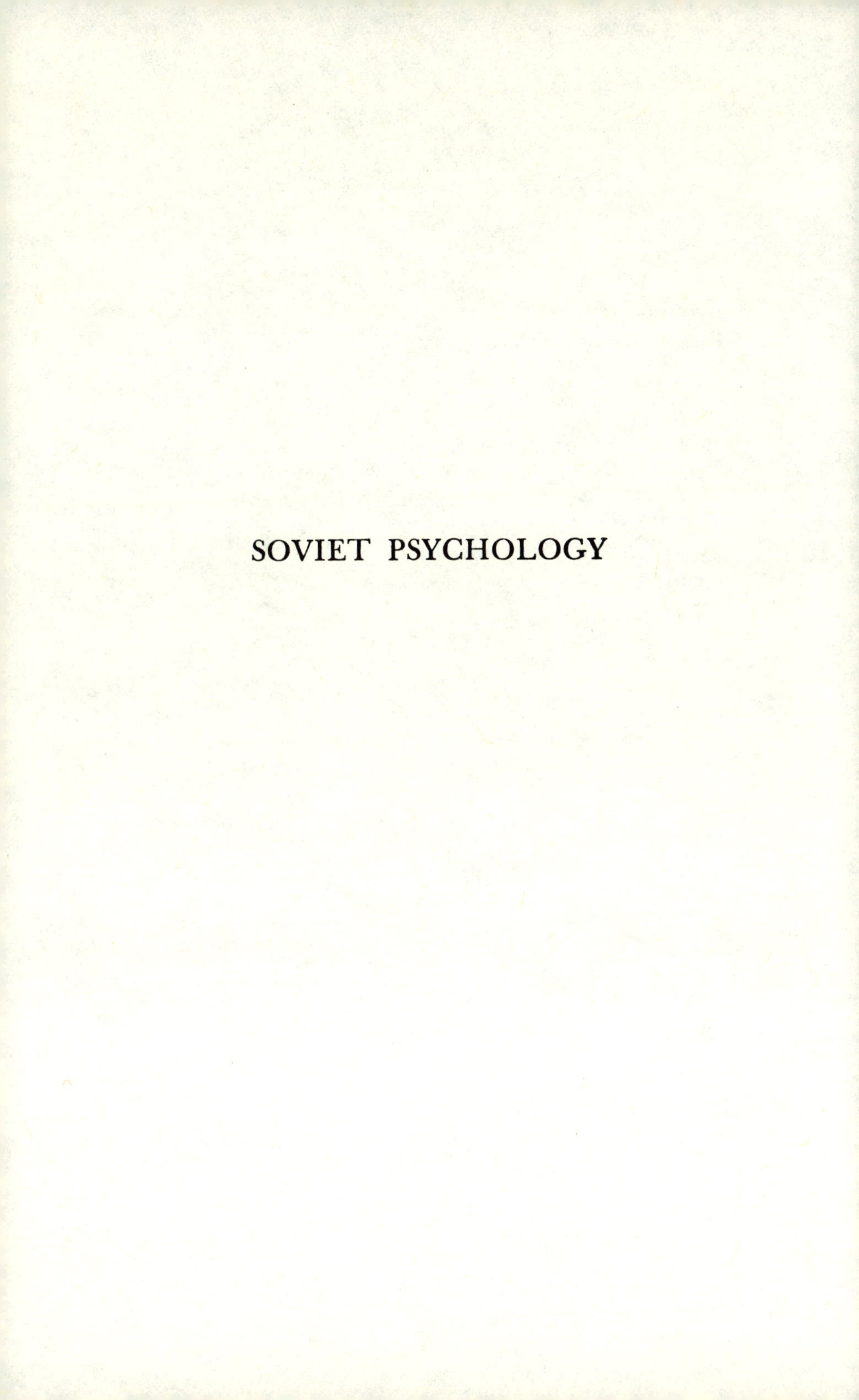

FOREWORD

Ralph B. Winn

During the last few years the American educators have
developed a considerable interest in the Soviet system of
education. The reason for that is that the Russians are
fast catching up with us in atomic physics, in the production of missiles, and in many other aspects of technology.
They are already graduating considerably more engineers
annually than our universities have ever graduated in
a single year. We are still ahead, on the whole, but the
margin of difference is steadily shrinking, and that means
a threat of bitter competition on the level of equality in
science, industry, international trade, and world politics.

For the first time in many years, our responsible scholars
look critically at our methods, techniques and achievements in education. Most of us are worried about our
shortage of teachers, from kindergarten to the graduate
school—the shortage which is apparently non-existent behind the iron curtain. We find that in many high schools
and colleges the traditional glamor of baseball and foot-
ball exists at the expense of the regular studies. We ac-
knowledge here and there that our students' motivation
for education leaves much to be desired, that it is selfishly
misdirected.

Some basic changes appear to be unavoidable. Our prominent educators already suggest numerous reforms in the educational procedures and curriculums. They agree on the whole that training in science and mathematics must be vastly improved. But the majority of the people, including our teachers, students and their parents, do not yet react at all. In their opinion, educational reforms, if needed, can wait. They have, indeed, other headaches to worry about, such as the current recession, segregation and desegregation, the new administration in Washington, international tensions and, of course, all kinds of personal problems. In a way, this is perfectly natural: our nation is prosperous, individualistic and freedom-loving.

But some well-informed persons say: "It may be later than you think!" The people ought to know that our future is no longer as secure as our past since the beginning of the century. They ought to realize that, for some reasons, admiration for the American way of life is being seriously questioned abroad. And at the root of all these recent developments lies our nineteenth-century school organization. Under these conditions, should we not ask and answer the simple question: Can we really afford to close our eyes to certain deficiencies of our educational habits, policies and patterns or, for that matter, to the shifting balance of power throughout the world?

If the people of this nation prefer to wait with educational reforms, the educated people themselves have a certain obligation of leadership. There is, no doubt, time enough to get thoroughly acquainted with the situation, to examine carefully our educational merits and demerits —and also what can be learned from other peoples, including the Russians. There is certainly no crime in learning. Indeed, it pays to know the truth wherever it is to be found. Even the truth which we happen to dislike is, after all, more valuable than the falsity we like.

Much can be learned—without any obligation to imitate—from the pages that follow, written (apart from the Introduction) by five prominent educators of the Soviet Union. The material is, to be sure, confined to one aspect only of the problem, namely, to the function of psychology in the growth and learning of children, particularly, while they attend school.

There are certain basic differences to be noted between the ways of American psychology and those of Soviet psychology, derived, no doubt, from the history of each nation and from respective philosophies of life. For instance, we have been greatly influenced by the behaviorist and psychoanalytic schools of thought, whereas the Russians will have nothing to do with them. They follow the lines of dialectical materialism. It is also somewhat surprising to discover that the Russian psychologists are completely unable to appreciate the value of our intelligence, aptitude and achievement tests. But that is their loss.

If we are willing to disregard some of these differences, much in the writing below becomes quite interesting and informative. It is instructive to learn, for instance, that the recent habit of our professional psychologists to shun the use of such familiar words as "consciousness," "mind," and even "experience" has not affected the Soviet psychologists at all. But the average American reader will hardly notice this peculiarity because, unlike our learned psychologists, he finds the above-mentioned words quite indispensable in thought and speech.

There are many wonderful passages in this book which

can be read without thinking of their foreign origin, for instance, the quite illuminating pages on "The Mental Development of Children of the Kindergarten Age" and "The Early School-Age Child" (both in A. N. Leontiev's *Intellectual Development of the Child*).

But most interesting of all is the idea going through the entire series of articles—something to be taken *very* seriously—that one of the principal tasks of the school, from its beginning, is to locate and promote among children talent of any creative type, for it is never too early to encourage future scientists, inventors, artists, writers, or plain workers to do their best and to learn and think unselfishly.

INTRODUCTION

Hans Hiebsch

The history of Soviet psychology has three distinct stages. The first begins with the October Revolution and ends in 1936. Its main characteristic was the struggle of the dictatorship of the proletariat against the tough and bitter resistance of the ideological bastions of the bourgeoisie. The latter maintained many positions, even after the victory of the proletariat was assured. Its main weapon in psychology and pedagogy was the so-called "paedology," about which something needs to be said.

It is obvious that a science like psychology, whose subject-matter is human consciousness, will influence, above all, those human activities which are concerned with the formation and creation of that consciousness, i.e., in education and its science, called pedagogy. Psychology is a science related to pedagogy and deals with a number of questions directly and indirectly concerned with education and instruction. Therefore, the psychology of childhood and youth was developed at the end of the 19th and the beginning of the 20th century as a separate discipline. It was born in the age of class war and imperialism, and bore from the very beginning the seed of fruitlessness, which must not be overlooked, even if one respects the rich experiences which it gathered. Its idealistic and metaphysical base precluded its development into a progressive and transforming science. The child psychology of the turn of the century and its philosophical and methodological base were turned, as early as 1896, into a special "science of the child," or paedology, founded by Chrisman under sponsorship of Wilhelm Rein. Paedology brewed together the facts of psychology, biology, physiology, etc. into a "science."

Paedology has this in common with the many different tendencies of bourgeois child psychology, that it views consciousness as independent from matter and as something primary, which develops, both in its phylogenesis and ontogenesis, "according to the law which started it on its course." The paedologists hold that the driving force of this development is either "heredity" or "environment" or a combination of both. But, in any case, these driving forces predetermine psychic development unalterably and fatalistically. The most important practical method of paedology is the test, which puts down, in each case, the stage of development reached and considered unalterable and necessary. Just as the child looks in the "snapshot" of the test, so it must look through the action of its heredity, or of the mechanical effect of its environment. It is a "hopeless diagnosis," a fruitless undertaking which, under capitalism, must inevitably lead to pessimism. For all that, paedology placed the child in the center of things by a romanticizing and sentimentalizing exaggeration of the love of the child, which it inherited from the bourgeois pedagogues. "The child" was the sun round which everything had to turn; everything had to start from "the child." The objective social tendencies of this entire conception are not dealt with here in any detail.

In the twenties, bourgeois paedology with its "pedagogical conclusions" found its way into the Soviet Union, and so did its practical consequences. The pupils were tested, sorted and differentiated. Special schools of all kinds were created for them, and the general standard of Soviet schools fell. . . .

In this first stage, paedology dominated almost completely the practice of psychology in the Soviet Union. And yet it was then that its defeat was prepared by the truly scientific investigations of I. P. Pavlov and the practical work of the best Soviet teachers. The hard conditions of ideological class warfare forged the great innovator of Soviet pedagogy, and therefore also of Soviet psychology, Anton Semyonovich Makarenko. His practical work, derived from the work of Socialist construction and driven by the consciousness of a fighting and unbending Communist, overcame in the twenties the paedological practices and the "theory" on which they were based. However, the theoreticians of the educational sciences were not yet able to draw from his victory the necessary conclusions. It was the Central Committee (C.C.) of the Communist Party of the Soviet Union (CPSU) which, after thorough discussions and investigations, drew these conclusions in its historical resolution of July 4, 1936 "On the paedological distortions in the system of the People's Commissariat for Education." This resolution marks the end of the first stage of the development of Soviet psychology.

In this resolution, the C.C. of the CPSU shows the practical consequences of the use of paedological work, theory and methods in Soviet schools: "An inflation of the system of special schools" for all kinds of different categories of difficult, retarded and defective children, in which "talented and gifted children were educated by the side of defective ones," which were selected "by the paedologists without any good reason on the basis of pseudo-scientific theories." The paedological method of differentiating the children "consisted essentially in pseudo-scientific experiments and the carrying out of innumerable investigations of pupils and parents in the form of senseless and harmful tests, i.e. in experiments which the party had condemned long ago."

Therefore, the C.C. of the CPSU condemned the theory and practice of the present-day so-called "paedology." It "is of the opinion that both theory and practice of so-called paedology rest on pseudo-scientific, un-Marxist assumptions . . . that such a theory could be formed only by an uncritical application in Soviet pedagogy of views and principles of unscientific bourgeois paedology, which has made it its task to prove, on the one hand, the special aptitudes and special rights to existence of the exploiting classes and of the "higher races" and, on the other hand, the physical and intellectual inferiority of the working classes and the "lower races," in order to uphold the rule of the exploiting class."

As a result of this resolution, the theory and practice of paedology were completely abolished in the Soviet Union.

The second stage, from 1936 to 1948, is characterized by the revival and more intensive utilization of the materialist traditions of the great Russian revolutionary democrats, philosophers and critics like Herzen, Belinsky, and Chernyshevsky. Moreover, it was then that the investigations of I. P. Pavlov, whose spiritual father had been the great 19th century Russian materialist physiologist Sechenov, became more and more influential. But the most important characteristic of this stage was intensive study of Marxism-Leninism by the scientists concerned.

The victory of T. D. Lysenko's biology in August 1948 marks the end of the second stage and the beginning of the third, in which Soviet psychology now finds itself. It studies the teachings of Marx and Engels, and Lenin; it uses dialectical materialism as its foundation; it practices criticism and self-criticism; it fights against bourgeois survivals and for the proletariat; it is a true science and on its way towards fulfilling Makarenko's motto: "Man must be changed "

THE DEVELOPMENT OF SOVIET PSYCHOLOGY

A. A. Smirnov

Psychology enjoys a respected and influential position in the Soviet Union. Men are the most valuable of all the fruits of this earth. Therefore, Soviet construction cares for men and devotes special attention to human personality. The relations between Soviet people are governed by socialist humanism. The psychic life and the psychic properties of human personality are the special concern of every Soviet citizen and one of the most important subjects of scientific study.

Soviet psychology is of decisive importance in solving problems of the education and instruction of the rising generation. Ushinsky, an outstanding Russian educationist and psychologist of the mid-19th century, said that "to be able to educate man in every way one must sufficiently know him in every way." The knowledge of the laws of the child's mental life and of its development is an indispensable condition for the solution of all pedagogical and didactical problems that are apt to arise. In this respect, Soviet psychology is a necessary constituent of the pedagogical sciences and has an important place in

11

their system.

The scientific theses worked out by Soviet psychology play an important part in developing the theory of Soviet pedagogy and the daily practice of Soviet education. They are widely taken into account in working out teaching plans and school programs, preparing textbooks, perfecting teaching methods, and carrying out the educational work of schools. Among the proofs of the wide recognition which the science of psychology enjoys in the Soviet Union are the following: the scientific work carried on with great vigor; the existence of a number of important institutions for psychological investigation, and the scientific work of the numerous chairs of psychology in Soviet universities. Particularly broad and many-sided is the work of the Moscow Psychological Institute of the Academy of Pedagogical Sciences; of the team led in Leningrad by Professor Ananiev; of the Ukrainian Psychological Institute under Professor Kostiuk; of the Georgian Psychological Institute under Usnadze; and of the Philosophical Institute of the Academy of Sciences of the USSR under Professor Rubinstein.

Psychology plays a very important part in the Soviet system of training the teachers. There are psychology courses in the curricula of all the Pedagogical Institutes and the Faculties of Humanities of all the universities. Special attention is paid to the practical psychological training of student-teachers. All these students take part in the practical psychological work of the school to which they are attached, during which they study individual pupils and their independent work, or the class collective as a whole, and analyze the content, methods and organization of the instruction hours from psychological points of view. These practical exercises are connected with the entire pedagogical work of the school, namely with the elaboration and execution of concrete pedagogical measures applied to pupils who are the subjects of the special study.

The training of psychologists is entrusted to special psychology departments which are part of several universities. Particular attention is devoted to the training of young scientists in the field of psychology, the so-called "aspirants." These are young people who received their higher education and proved their interest and aptitude for independent scientific work. They now receive an additional three years' training in psychology, including an acquaintance with the nature of scientific investigation.

Another proof of the importance of psychology in the Soviet Union is its teaching in secondary schools. It is here a subject which plays a specially important part in the educational work of the school. It acquaints the pupils of the upper classes of the school with the laws of psychology, and thus fosters in them the development of the materialist world view, an understanding of the mental life of others, the formation of valuable personality traits and the organization of their own independent schoolwork. The pupils show, in turn, great interest in the psychology classes; their practical value is obvious to them.

What are the theoretical bases of Soviet psychology? It is founded, first of all, on . . . the teaching of dialectical materialism. Its most important task is to develop the fundamental theses of that teaching in the sphere of man's experience. The history of psychology, like that of other sciences, is the history of the conflict between materialism and idealism. All progressive thinkers were adherents of the materialist theory, while idealism always provided a foundation of reactionary views. It not only hampered the progress of sciences, but was an obstacle to their very formation. We define idealism as all philosophical theories according to which the psychic factor is something autonomous and independent of matter; i.e., it is not a special property of matter, nor is it a product of the brain. We define materialism, on the contrary, as all the theories which start from the assumption that the psychic factor has no independent existence, but is only a property of matter and is formed in the long process of its development. Since idealism accepted the psychic factor as independent, it attempted to explain the entire mental life from out of itself, from the laws of the psyche. In doing this, it ignored the most important fact which is offered by our knowledge of the dependence of experience on the nervous system and the outside world: namely, that consciousness is itself only a property of matter, a product of the brain, and that it develops as a result of the action of an objective reality which is outside us and independent of us.

Idealism could not and would not understand that consciousness is merely a reflection, an image in us of the real world. It could or would not understand that the social relations between men are the most important among the factors of objective reality that influence us, and that these relations are determined by the material living conditions of the society. It also ignored the fact that these relations are shaped quite differently in different historical eras, depending in each case on the material living conditions of the society in question. Idealism could or would not see the class character of consciousness in a class society, the dependence of the mental life of men on the class of each individual and on whether he belongs to the ruling or the exploited class.

Nor could the pre-Marxist, mechanistic materialism offer an adequate explanation of man's experience. This materialism has the characteristic trait of trying to explain the psychic processes and consciousness by purely physiological or even physical and chemical processes. It saw the qualitative peculiarity of the psychic processes not as a special property of highly developed matter, created during its development. Neither mechanistic materialism nor idealism managed to understand the dependence of consciousness on the growth of man's social life, on his way of living and on his class affiliation. Mechanistic materialism had no understanding of the active role of consciousness of progressive ideas in changing reality. This materialism finally mechanized man's entire life and turned him into an automaton.

The so-called vulgar materialism of Büchner, Vogt and Moleschott was particularly far removed from a positive and scientific understanding of psychic life. Contemporary mechanistic theories are also quite incapable of a correct understanding of man's mental life. This is especially true of American behaviorism, which tries to replace psychology, the science of consciousness, by a psychology conceived as a science of behavior; the latter being understood as the sum of mechanically produced reactions. Applied to instruction and education, these theories lead to a denial of the need of a conscious acquisition of knowledge and skills and also of a conscious discipline and activity for the child. Instruction and education thus become mere drill or mechanical training—which is the position of Thorndike and some other behaviorists. The mechanists deny with particular obstinacy the need of consciousness in the instruction and education of the youngest children and of pupils of elementary schools. They thus become the champions of reactionary class interests, for the elementary school is a mass school, accessible to all the strata of the population, while the higher levels of education are accessible only to the children of the rich. The behaviorists thus rob the children of the poor of the possibility to learn consciously, and expose them only to an education that is more or less mechanistic. . . . This reduces the future workers to mere robots.

Only dialectical materialism has a correct conception of the nature of experience. It proved that mental life is a special property of highly organized matter, which consists in representing the material world. It alone offered the proof of the social conditioning of human consciousness and of its dependence on social relations which are, in their turn, determined by the material living conditions of each society. It alone emphasized the historical nature of consciousness and revealed the class character of consciousness in a class society. It alone has the correct idea of the effective role of consciousness and of the importance of progressive ideas in the life of society.

What are the chief problems that occupy Soviet psychology? The problem of personality has a very important position in its system. The aim of the investigations of Soviet psychologists is, after all, man in concrete, the living human personality. The chief task of Soviet psychology is to uncover the mental properties of man and the laws of his mental development. How does Soviet psychology solve this problem? It decisively rejects all theories which argue that man's personality and experience are determined by biological, natural drives. Such a conception assumes the immutability, i.e., "eternity" of the basic psychic qualities of a person. However, history, and especially the practice of socialist construction, have taught us that the mental qualities of men are very changeable. The years since the Revolution have wrought radical changes in the personality qualities of Soviet people. Individualism has yielded to collectivism and new capacities for patriotism and organization have been revealed. It is absolutely false to claim, as the personality theory of depth psychology does, that the influence of social and historical conditions operates through an upper part of human personality, which is opposed by a lower part, consisting of natural drives. Actually, the social influences embrace the entire personality of man and determine from the beginning his whole mental life. Man even satisfies his organic needs depending on the social influence to which he is subjected. This is the essential difference between man and animal: the experience of animals is determined by biological factors; that of man by social and historical conditions of life. The individualistic strivings, which depth psychology assumes to be natural and inborn drives, are viewed by Soviet psychology as in no way inborn but formed under the influence of certain definite social conditions.

But what are these conditions? The answer to these questions must start from the following thesis: Human society is, at any stage of its development, a class society. In such a society, man always belongs to a certain class and lives under conditions that are characteristic of his class. The influences to which he is subjected, always emanate from a certain class; man's mental life in a class society therefore has a class character.

In a capitalist society, the ruling class has pronounced individualistic strivings and interests. And so a decidedly individualistic psychology is typical of it. This psychology arises from economic conditions characterized by private property. The bourgeoisie tries to explain its individualistic and egotistic strivings as the unchangeable and basic qualities of human nature. But the only reason for this explanation is to justify the capitalistic order and to prove that this order corresponds to the allegedly innate egotistic strivings of man. Actually, the capitalistic order does not arise from these allegedly innate economic strivings of man. The real situation is rather the reverse: the individualistic psychology of man arises from the capitalistic order and, wherever that order is liquidated, the egotistic strivings disappear in the end.

In a socialist society, the personal strivings of man are not opposed to the interests of society, but agree with them. Personal interests are therefore not repressed in such a society but, on the contrary, reach their full expression and development here, because they fully correspond to the interest of society. One fact at least can be used as an example. The motivation of the choice of vocation by Soviet youth is, naturally, personal since everyone chooses the vocation that suits him. There exist, in this respect, no restrictions in our country. However, Soviet youth is also guided in its choice of vocation by the idea of being of the best possible use to its country, and this social motivation is essential for our young people. Motives like desire for material se-

18

curity or a "high" social position are totally absent in them. They know that, in their country, every vocation gives material security, and can lead to high honors and a position of dignity. The honorable title of "Hero of the Socialist Fatherland" is granted to men and women of all vocations who achieve successes in their chosen type of work. This harmony of personal and social interests, and their very unity, proves how wrong the theories are which assure us that social influence can manifest itself only as the suppression of the personal strivings of man.

Among such theories is, in addition to some tendencies of depth psychology, the theory of Freud. What we have already said fully justifies us in rejecting theories based on certain "depth strata" of personality. Their inacceptability is also justified by the fact that they consider biological needs or the "subconscious," and not reason and consciousness, to be the determining factors of human personality. Consciousness is regarded by them as merely an instrument for the satisfaction of these needs. But consciousness is actually the highest form of psychic life and the highest stage of its development. Man is not characterized by the dominion of dark forces of the instincts or of the subconscious, but rather by the dominion of his reason which reflects the world clearly and correctly. We therefore consider the highest aim of education to be the development of consciousness and the placing of the entire behavior under the rule of consciousness. Instincts and the subconscious push man back, reason leads him forward. Whoever wants to fight for progressive ideas, for a bright future of mankind, must reject the theories which hold that the psychic foundation of man consists of instinctive, in-

19

born or unconscious strivings. All attempts to uphold such theories and to justify the conditioning of man by instinctive and unconscious strivings, are in the service of reaction. It is not for nothing that fascism has made much use of such theories.

The problem of aptitude occupies in the Soviet Union a special position among the problems of the psychology of personality. How has Soviet psychology solved this problem? The great unfolding of talents among the Soviet people has proved for all time the falsity of the reactionary "theory" of the special aptitudes of the exploiting classes and of the so-called "higher" races. It also confirmed the truth of Lenin's words on the organizational talents slumbering in the people: "There is a lot of organizational talent among the people, i.e. the workers and the working peasants. But they are repressed, corrupted and eliminated by the thousands under capitalism, and, we do not know yet how to find them, encourage them and put them on their feet. (Author's note: Lenin said this in the first years of Soviet rule.) But we shall learn to do it, when we set out to learn with the full revolutionary enthusiasm, without which there can be no victorious revolution." These words of Lenin must, of course, be understood to refer not only to organizational talents but to all kinds of talent. The practice of Socialist construction in the Soviet Union has proved sufficiently the truth of these words. It has thus refuted all lying and unscientific theories which attempt to prove the right to existence and the special privileges of the exploiting classes and the "higher" races. It also refutes all theories of the mental and intellectual inferiority of the working classes and the "lower" races. It has been proved that the working masses of the Soviet Union, and in particular the peoples retarded by the Tsarist and capitalist yoke, can be raised to a high cultural level by the changing of their social and economic living conditions.

Soviet psychology rejects the assumption of directly inborn abilities. Only certain anatomical and physiological characteristics of the organism, and especially of the nervous system, can be inborn in this sense. Abilities are always the product of a development which takes place under certain definite social conditions, under certain quite concrete forms of human activity and in the course of a long process of instruction and education. The peculiarities of the nervous system are always explicable in several different ways. Given the same starting conditions, the result of the development, as expressed in the abilities achieved, will be quite different, corresponding to the differing conditions and forms of education and instruction.

Soviet psychology assumes that the successful execution of any ability is based on all kinds of combinations of individual abilities. The loss of any special ability can never be an obstacle to achieving outstanding success in any sphere, for highly developed abilities can sucessfully replace other and less well developed ones. This possibility of a mutual compensation of abilities is extraordinarily great. Soviet psychology rejects the pseudo-scientific pretension to measure ability or talent in any form and considers its main tasks to be the analysis of qualitative characteristics of aptitude and the discovery of methods for the successful development of abilities. This is why we Soviet psychologists investigate abilities of all kinds. Our investigations have already opened up very rich possibilities of developing abilities through teaching and educational influences.

Why does Soviet psychology reject the quantitative measurement of abilities and, in particular, the method of tests which is so widely applied by American psychologists? It rejects this method because it is founded on a fatalistic theory of aptitudes which considers human abilities predetermined through heredity and unchangeable by environment. In this way, it denies the existing rich possibilities of development. This kind of theory assumes that it is possible, by measuring abilities at a certain time, to determine the suitability of men for future forms of activity. The tests are given a prognostic value which they actually do not possess. It cannot be determined, without any further ado, from the way in which a man's abilities express themselves at any given time, how they will behave in the future. The possibility of their development is, in any case, extraordinarily great and it must be, moreover, remembered that abilities develop during and with the activities of man. They are even, to an important extent, the result of the activity for which they are required and not the assumption or condition of the successful execution of such an activity. When an activity is executed, the abilities required for it develop in man. The influence of instruction and education plays a most important part in this respect. This is why the most important task of the teacher is to develop the abilities of his pupils. The fatalistic theories, on which the test method is based, deprive him of this task. When we pass, on the basis of tests, a judgment that is essentially fatalistic, we deprive the teacher of the possibility to explore all possible ways and methods of developing the abilities of his pupils.

22

The tests have neither a prognostic nor a diagnostic value. They are not even capable of giving a true characterization of the abilities that happen to be actually present at the moment of testing. Why do they fail to do so? The successful performance of an activity, the solution of a problem, do not depend on abilities alone. They also depend on the underlying motivation, on what drives us towards the solution of the problem. A simple fact will explain what we mean. An investigation proved that the capacity of memorization of children of pre-school age is influenced by motivation. The following experiments were made. In the first case, the children were asked to memorize certain words in the course of a play period. The children played at "kindergarten." One child took over the job of buying in a store certain things required by the kindergarten. In the second case, the children were asked to memorize the same words not in the course of a play period, but of an ordinary experiment, conducted in the way common to such experiments. The result was that the children memorized twice as many words in the first case as in the second. Why? Because the motives of memorization were not the same.

The tests do not take into account the motives of human actions. Moreover, the motives of the children submitted to a test can be quite varied. Therefore, the results of the tests can never be quite correct, not because of differing abilities of the children, but merely because the children have quite different relations to the solution of the problems presented to them in the test.

The psychology of bourgeois countries has developed complicated procedures to help determine the diagnostic value of tests. It uses for the purpose the statistics of variations and obtains a quantitative determination of the correlation between the results of the investigation and successfully performed action. The authors of the tests seem to be satisfied if the limit of error is low.

But Soviet psychology can never be satisfied with such a solution. It invokes the principles of humanism and therefore cannot accept even rare errors. After all, behind every error there is a living human being, a living child and his fate. This is by no means a matter of no consequence to a Soviet psychologist. He cannot offer his sanction to such an error, not even in a single case.

Why then is the test method so widely proclaimed in capitalist countries? Because its results are used to serve political, reactionary class aims. Such tests are used to prove that the level of ability is lower in children of workers and peasants than in children of the propertied classes, and that the abilities of children of subject peoples are lower than those of children of the so-called "higher" peoples and "higher" races. These tests serve as foundation for the assertion that social inequality is based on and justified by such differences of aptitude. Actually, it is not social inequality that is caused by such differences in aptitude, but the different possibilities of developing abilities are caused by the social and economic inequality of men in capitalist society. If, in capitalist countries, the children of workers achieve worse results in tests than the children of property owners, it is not because they are less gifted but because they were greatly hampered in developing their abilities by their conditions of life, determined by the oppression, exploitation and social and economic inequality prevailing in these countries.

If we reject the method of tests and measurements, does this mean that we do not think it is necessary to investigate the abilities of the pupils? No, we do not believe this. But we hold that a correct investigation of abilities is possible only if the child's activities are performed under his ordinary conditions of life, and when his abilities are not investigated statistically but in their development and change, in connection with the whole personality of the child, his instruction and education, his entire life.

Such an investigation can be carried out by the teacher himself. He can investigate the child in all the forms of his activity and under the most varied conditions, and he can follow the change and development of his abilities. He must have an adequate knowledge of the child's whole life, of the conditions of his development and the peculiarities of his personality. Soviet teachers give a high importance to this task and perform it in their practical pedagogical activity.

One of the most important theses of Soviet psychology —and also one of its most important problems—is the theory of the unity of man's consciousness and activity. Soviet psychologists believe that individual aspects of mental life must not be studied in the abstract, but in connection with the concrete activities of men. Thus, thinking, memory and attention cannot be studied by themselves, but only under the conditions of an activity, during teaching, work, etc. The subject of the investigations of Soviet psychologists is not the child's thinking in itself, but the process of his thinking in the solution of mathematical problems, in applying the rules of spelling, in learning literary or scientific texts. Soviet psychologists do not investigate the memory processes by themselves, but the memorization of the varied materials offered to the pupil in the course of his instruction. They do not study the formation and growth of concepts in the way of, e.g. Narziss Ach, who investigated the formation of artificial concepts created by himself. They note how the pupils handle scientific concepts which are explained to them in the course of their schoolwork. Such a method of investigation is the only way to make psychology a true, living and concrete science, with wide possibilities of practical application. This is the way which Soviet psychology has taken.

The theory of the unity of consciousness and activity places before Soviet psychologists the very important task of giving a psychological analysis of concrete human activity. In this connection, particular attention is given to creative activity. The subject of investigation is, above all, the creative activity of the worker in production. In the Soviet Union, the worker is not a mere appendage of the machine. He is the creator of new and more perfected working methods, the organizer of the process of production, the designer and the inventor. The new, Communist attitude towards work, conditioned by the new production relations and the disappearance of the exploitation of man by man, produced entirely new forms of work. The activity of the workers became a creative work. This was expressed with the greatest clarity in the activity of the Stakhanovites. Their creative work is a most important subject of psychological investigation. In the sphere of psychology of work, the investigators are faced with the very important problems of discovering the psychological requirements of different professions. This is not a matter of investigating aptitudes for different kinds of work, but of studying the conditions under which, within the work of the profession, the necessary personal conditions are created, under which the work itself educates and changes the worker. A considerable number of studies of Soviet psychologists is devoted to the investigation of the creative work of artists—painters, musicians, actors and also writers. This is also true of the work of scientists and inventors.

Particular attention is paid to the investigation of the learning process, especially of the schoolwork of pupils of elementary and secondary schools. These are the problems that form the main content of Soviet educational psychology.

No less important in the work of Soviet psychology are the problems of the psychology of growth, and especially the problems of the child's mental development. A question is raised in this connection which is so important that it deserves some detailed treatment. It is the question of our attitude to the peculiarities of growing children's behavior. In solving this question Soviet psychology starts from the thesis that the peculiarities of each age are not to be viewed as unchangeable and eternal characteristics of that age, independent of the concrete conditions of the child's life. Soviet psychology refers here to the social conditioning of the development of man and his consciousness. It proclaims the assertion that the peculiarities of the various ages depend on social and historical conditions under which the child's life, activities, instruction and education take place. If these conditions are changed, the specific age peculiarities also change. The correctness of this thesis is clearly proved by the remarkable changes in Soviet children under the influence of the new social conditions of life. Instruction and education must not therefore be built on some "eternal" characteristics of each age, but rather must start from concrete facts formed under some definite social and historical conditions. They must also bear in mind their possible further development and growth, of which the child is capable at a given age, and the increase and intensification of that child's intellectual forces.

The Soviet psychologists hold themselves entitled to assert, on the basis of the many investigations they carried out in the field of child psychology, that many concepts held by bourgeois psychologists concerning the nature of children do not correspond to reality. Among these erroneous concepts are the theses of Stern about the step-by-step development of the capacity for observation; Piaget's thesis of the egocentricity of childish thought; the characterization of childish memory, and many others. All these theses do not do justice to the possibilities which slumber in each child of that age grade. They underestimate the growth possibilities of the child and distort the true picture of the child's mental development.

Among the erroneous concepts mentioned above is the thesis of the allegedly inevitable crises which accompany some stages of the child's development, notably puberty. The reports of Soviet investigators and the educational practice of the Soviet family and school show, however, that these crises can be completely avoided when the child is instructed and educated in the right way and his life is lived under favorable social and historical conditions.

Since Soviet psychology denies the immutability of

28

the child's age peculiarities, it must also decisively reject the norms which are used to measure the child's intellectual forces and to determine the step-by-step process of his development.

What are the methods used by Soviet psychologists in their work? The basic principle to which we refer all questions of method is this: we do not confine ourselves to any single method, but apply many and quite different ones. Our attention is concentrated on studying the processes that are of interest to us in the actual life of the child or under conditions which closely approximate the ordinary conditions of that life. We therefore make a wide use of the method of observation and live experiment, i.e., an experiment that is closely linked with the process of teaching and the pupil's work at school. Where it is a question of individual peculiarities, we try to obtain as complete information as possible about every pupil in order to understand the quality of his mental process in connection with the other sides of his personality.

In all such investigations, we are interested not only in the results of the individual processes of behavior, but also in the way they take place. Thus, for example, we are not only interested in finding out how much a pupil memorizes under different conditions of learning. We are also interested in the way in which he memorizes, in what he does to memorize, and in the course of the memorization process itself. We devote special attention to the qualitative aspect of the processes we study.

I would like to make the following concluding remark. Soviet psychology, like all Soviet sciences, works under conditions that are extremely favorable to its development and growth. It is given the greatest attention and care, and the government offers it large economic means for the realization of its work. Soviet educationists are given a chance to do a broadly conceived and many-sided scientific work. They form a scientific collective of men working together in a comradely fashion. They are linked by their general tasks and by their aims, which are: to give an objectively correct explanation of the laws of development of man's life and consciousness; to reveal the real motives of human actions; to show the rich possibilities of growth of man's intellectual forces; to provide better methods for the instruction and education of children; and to foster the formation of valuable personality traits. Soviet psychologists discuss their scientific problems in the widest possible way.

THE PRESENT TASKS OF
SOVIET PSYCHOLOGY

A. N. Leontiev

Psychology is not a part of the system of biological sciences. But it is very closely connected with the physiology of the higher nervous activity and animal psychology, i.e., the science of the development of living creatures. The problem of heredity also closely touches upon human psychology.

The theories of the American biologist Morgan found their strongest expression in the work on animal psychology by V. M. Borovski. In his last publication, Borovski stated that a direct influence of external conditions on the heredity of living creatures is possible only through the action of factors which influence mutations, e.g., X-rays. The theory that "a new milieu can not only change the characteristics of an individual but also influence it in such a way that the changed peculiarities are exhibited in its descendants," i.e., the theory of the mutability of the hereditary mass under the influence of new living conditions, is described by Borovski as the remnant of "a once widespread theory," as factually false and logically improbable. "There is no inheritance of acquired characteristics," writes Borovski.[1] He adds to his statement the traditional argument: "The descendants of fishes whose tailfins were cut off, do not exhibit the expected abbreviation."[2]

This false, metaphysical conception of the immutability of characteristics of living creatures hindered the solution of numerous problems of animal psychology, especially those of instinct. Darwin inaugurated the scientific treatment of these problems. He was interested in the importance of instinct in the life of the species and reached the realization that the development of species can only be understood by assuming the inheritability of the changes made under the influence of new conditions of life that did not correspond to the existing instincts.[3]

The Morganists of today distort Darwin's theory when they proclaim that the inheritance of acquired characteristics is incompatible with a correct conception of the instincts.[4] They thus throw overboard the important contribution of Darwin which differentiates between instinct and the ability to perform a given action.

The textbook of "General Foundations of Psychology," by S. L. Rubinstein, develops a false, objectivist view of the problem of inheritance and variability. The author does, indeed, defend the correct view of the decisive role of the environment, but also proclaims the erroneous view that the question of the influence of the environment in the phylogenetic development of living creatures can remain an open one. Thus Rubinstein presents the theories of the Morganists and of Lysenko as equally important, although they are actually diametrically opposed.[5] The theories of Morgan, Weismann and Mendel were much quoted and applied in the So-

32

viet Union until the Central Committee of the Communist Party of the Soviet Union passed the resolution of July 4, 1936. This resolution which condemned paedology, i.e., the science of the special psychology of the child, also put an end to the "two-factor theory" which proclaimed the equal role of heredity and environment. . . .

In the last years, a correct view of the problem of heredity asserted itself in the work of Soviet psychologists, especially as regards the decisive importance of education in the development of human personality. But the concrete questions on the nature of inherited tendencies, their mutability and their importance for the mental development of man, have hardly been dealt with so far. We can therefore point to only a very limited number of psychological studies which reach concrete solutions of such questions.

First of all, we must mention the studies of B. M. Teplov on the problem of inborn tendencies and on the development of abilities. Teplov further develops the important idea that only anatomical and physiological characteristics of the organism can be inborn. These can not be described as abilities; for abilities develop only in the process of the corresponding activities and are therefore dependent on the objective conditions which make these activities possible.[6]

It must, however, be emphasized that these and other psychological studies which deal with the problem of inherited human characteristics and their role in the development of the mental factor, are merely the first steps towards a scientific clarification. The theory of inheritance and variability of vegetable and animal organisms cannot be mechanically transferred to human psychology. This does not mean, however, that psychology can avoid the problem of tendencies. On the contrary, psychology now faces the imperative task of providing the theoretical foundations for the solution of this problem.

*   *
*

The triumph of creative Soviet Darwinism, as expressed in the complete victory of the Michurinist tendency in the Soviet Union, also meant the foundation of a dialectical materialist theory of the development of living organisms. . . . The phylogenetic theory of Michurin and Lysenko has also been applied to psychology. . . .

The most important problems of mental development are the questions of the historical development of man and of the individual development of the child. Two conceptions are diametrically opposed in connection with these questions: the idealistic and the dialectical materialistic.

The metaphysical-idealistic conception views the development of the mental factor as a process of the unfolding of intellectual abilities inherent in man. The living conditions of man form only a background to this process. They make the abilities apparent and direct their development to one side or another, into one direction or another. Such a conception is characteristic of the bourgeois psychology.

It is very closely linked with the tendency of bourgeois psychology to view the mental factor not historically but as something abstract, unhistorical and "gene-

34

rally human." But the so-called "generally human" characteristics of the factor are actually nothing but the characteristics of present-day man in a class society. The mental character of the members of the exploiting class becomes particularly apparent in this connection. The mental character of members of the exploited classes and of oppressed peoples is considered not to be up to standard and is explained through its primitive nature.

This conception of man became especially clear when reactionary psychologists openly entered into the service of military imperialism. They tried to prove in their writings that elementary psychological phenomena like work for payment or the love of money also had an eternal validity. Their rudiments could be experimentally proved to exist in anthropoid apes. Innumerable experiments were made to "prove" that human actions ultimately express only those needs, tendencies and instincts that are rooted in the "depths" of personality, and that the highest drives of men were merely a strange kind of "superstructure" above these "depths" and merely one of their manifestations. The primitive needs and motivations were therefore the strongest. "Thus, punishments and the need to satisfy hunger or the sex drive are stronger motivations than those of a social character"—we read in a survey of results of investigations made abroad, published in an American psychological journal. It is even assumed that the most important needs and emotions are immutable in man—as is emphasized by John Dewey. Since this erroneous view of the strength of biological factors is also extended to social phenomena, the foreign reactionary psychology reaches highly backward conclusions. It is enough here to say that this psychology attributed the origin of German-Fascist bestiality to ". . . the hysterical and paranoid tendencies of Hitler and Rosenberg" to which "the nation merely reacted in the same way."[7]

The progressive Soviet psychology considers the historical development of the mental factor from theoretical positions that are diametrically opposite. Soviet psychologists start from the Marxist thesis that the consciousness of man is social and historical in its nature, that it is determined by social existence and that it changes qualitatively with changes in social and economic conditions. They explain the peculiarities of the mental factor not by so-called eternal properties of human nature, but by the objective living conditions of man in society. Contrary to bourgeois psychology, Soviet psychology develops as a kind of social science, as the science of the experience of concrete and historical men.

The psychological characteristics of human personality are viewed not as the product of the interaction of two extremely opposed principles, i.e., the biological and the social, or heredity and environment, but as the product of the development of human life and activity under the given social relations. The development process of the mental factor is thus not conceived as a process that is put into motion by external forces and elements, but as one which has as its driving force the inner contradictions of human life in society itself.

But life itself, the child's activity which determines in its course his mental development, is not spontaneous—it is under the influence of education and instruction. In a Socialist society, which does not develop spontaneously but is directed by men, education is the decisive force which forms man intellectually. It must correspond to the aims and the needs of the entire society, of the entire people or, in other words, it must fully agree with real human needs, and also with those of individual man.

These theoretical conceptions of the development of the mental factor are characteristic of Soviet psychology. But it must by no means be concluded from this that Soviet psychology already possesses a fully developed Marxist theory of the historical development of the factor. It must, on the contrary, be stated that this problem has so far received an inadequate treatment. We still have no fundamental research into these questions. The few studies that do exist, like the "General Foundations of Psychology" by S. L. Rubinstein and the "Sketch of the Psychological Development" by A. N. Leontiev, suffer, as was noted in scientific criticism, from considerable defects.

And so the most important task that now faces the Soviet psychologists is the creation of a historical psychology, a theory of the historical development of the mental factor at different stages of society and in representatives of different social classes, of the basic changes in human experience produced by the abolition of private property and by the planned transformation of this experience under conditions of gradual transition from socialism to communism.

*   *

*

Soviet psychology has done much more thorough work

on the ontological development of the mental factor, i.e., on its development in the process of life. This is a central problem of child psychology and one of great practical importance.

In a theory of child psychology we must, of course, also start from a consideration of the driving forces in the development of the child's experience. Contrary to the metaphysical theory of "two-factors" (i.e., heredity and environment), according to which the development of the child's psyche is said to proceed fatalistically, Soviet psychology shows that this development is based on the growth of the child's living conditions and of his activities, which are determined by objective living conditions and education.

The child enters the society of men with his very first steps into life. He learns from society the activities which it has developed and the language which reflects the social practices of mankind. The child's environment presents him with all kinds of tasks and demands and thus actively makes him engage in activities required by these tasks and demands. Thus, the social environment instructs and educates the child.

This does not happen without a conscious setting by society of the aims of education and instruction. This conscious and purposeful process of education, which starts in early childhood, is continued, though in essentially different forms, in the kindergarten, at school and in social life. The mental development of the child is realized in this process.

Numerous investigations by Soviet psychologists on the development of mental processes of children, e.g., of perception, memory, thought and speech, have given concrete proofs that the formation of these processes must not be viewed as the unfolding of innate abilities under the influence of all kinds of conditions of the milieu. This formation takes place in the course of the child's directed activities. The psychological characteristics that were hitherto fatalistically attributed to given stages of development, proved to be actually the products of the child's life which went on under certain definite social conditions, the product of the child's instruction and education. Rich possibilities of producing desirable psychological and character traits in the children were thus revealed.

This does not, of course, mean that the general course of the child's mental development is not subject to a certain law, and that education is independent from the child's age and from the stage of development he has reached. To be able to direct the child's psychological development, one must be acquainted with its course and its respective stages. It is therefore necessary to deal once more fundamentally with the problem of the stages of the child's psychological development.

The numerous periodisations, i.e., lists of stages, of childhood of bourgeois psychology are well known. All of them start, more or less, from the metaphysical conception of psychological development as an unfolding of the child's innate characteristics, i.e., from theories which falsely transfer so-called biological laws into child psychology. They identify the psychological with the biological development of the child, and use such phenomena as change of teeth or the development of the function of the sexual glands, to mark the stages. All these periodisations are attempts to present the psychological development of the child as a phenomenon of growth.

The pseudo-scientific character of these periodisations, which are essentially paedological, is obvious. It is our task to oppose them by a periodisation of the child's growth that is founded on the dialectical materialist conception of development. The solution of this problem was made possible by the investigations, already mentioned, of individual mental processes in the child and by studies of the development of various kinds of child activities—play, learning, work, etc.

The study of the concrete activities of the child made it possible to link qualitatively differentiable stages of the psychological development with the most important forms of activity in the various periods of the child's life. At the same time it could be shown that, at each stage of the development of any kind of activity, other and more complicated forms of that activity were being prepared, which will eventually assume the leading role in the following stage. It was also shown that each stage of development already prepares the leap-like transition to the following stage, and that this transition is necessary and regular. This discovery provides a new foundation for the successive periods of the child's psychological development: these depend on the activities which determine in each case the child's life and on the typical relations of social life that link the child with other people and mark his position in society.

To take one example, at the stage of development that starts with the child's entry into school, learning at school is his most important activity. It reflects a new type of life relations into which the child enters. By this activity, the child acquires a new position in society of which he becomes conscious, namely that of a Soviet pupil.

40

Learning is, under the given conditions, the first socially important activity that is binding upon the child and is fixed by law. The quality of the pupil's work at school is the subject of an objective evaluation by society. It determines the relationship of the environment to the pupil and creates for him a certain definite position in his school and in his class: he becomes a good or bad pupil. With his new duties, the pupil also acquires new rights. He can claim from his environment that it should give him help and that it should grant him a considerable degree of independence. He passes into a new form of life, which he finds in the collective of his class and his school. At the same time, important changes take place in the child's intellectual development through the process of instruction. His memory and his thinking change; and he develops an ability of continuous and systematic thought. He takes part in the complicated relations of his new collective life, which form in him special moral ideas and sentiments.

This example shows that the contents of the stages of the child's development are not unchangeable, but depend on the social conditions under which he lives and which make possible the varying contents of his life and activity. The stages of psychological development can therefore differ in their social conditions, for all their regular succession. At the same stage of development, one set of social conditions may require a transition to systematic schooling, and another a transition to systematic work.

The problem of the transitions from one stage of psychological development to another is particularly important. These transitions occur in this way: essential changes occur in the psychological processes of the preceding stage which are linked with the child's activities. They prepare the transition to a more complex form of life and the appearance of a new leading activity. The transition is not gradual but leaplike.

Our educational task consists in directing the child's development in such a way that what he has achieved in the previous stage is continued according to plan so as to develop in the child qualities that will be of a decisive importance in the next stage. In other words, it is necessary to orient oneself not only by the existing possibilities of the child but also by the perspective of his further development. The transition to a new sphere of life relationships, to a new "position" in life, must not occur spontaneously but must be directed by education. The child must be presented in time with new tasks and included in a new sphere of relationships. Otherwise, this transition becomes a "crisis of development," i.e. a process which is erroneously attributed by bourgeois psychology to an "age of transition," as its necessary feature.

The studies of the child's psychological development are by no means completed. The false metaphysical conception is not yet overcome, and we still come across it here and there in our psychology. It makes its appearance in the question of the interrelationship between psychology and pedagogy, e.g. in K. N. Kornilov. He does, indeed, emphasize the necessity of pedagogy to take into account, in educating the will, "the requirements of a concrete historical epoch," "the family conditions of the child's life" and "the moral abilities." But he also says that, for the psychological analysis of the act of will, "all this is in no way binding," and he closes his account with this statement: "The psychologist who occupies himself with the problem of educating the will, ceases to be a psychologist and becomes a pedagogue."[8]

Kornilov's point of view represents a retreat to theoretical conceptions which isolate the mental factor from education and from life. They do not view it as the product of life, but, on the contrary, as its precondition which provides the child—and the man—with the possibility of satisfying the requirements of instruction, education and life.

These false tendencies sometimes manifest themselves in the ways of satisfying the requirements of pedagogy with regard to the so-called age stages. We mean the requirements which the pedagogue needs for the organization of his educational work. These requirements are sometimes falsely understood so as to show only the existing "level" of the psychological development, but not the perspective of that development and—what should be most important—the actual laws of formation of the higher functions. Only these latter foster the pedagogical activity and the further improvement of the methods of education.

These considerations emphasize, of course, the task of exploring the psychological development of the child. But they also emphasize the problem of linking psychology and practice, and in particular, the pedagogic practice of education and instruction, in a new way.

*　　*

*

The most important lesson to be drawn from the results of the Lysenko discussion of the Lenin Academy of Agricultural Sciences is the need to subordinate the development of progressive science to the tasks of progressive

43

Socialist practice. A true scientific theory cannot be developed without a close connection with practice.

This lesson is of special importance to psychology. Bourgeois psychology which, especially as regards ideology, carries out the orders of the ruling class, has turned away more and more from the solution of really practical problems, and busies itself essentially with imaginary problems.

But even when it solved practical problems, bourgeois psychology remained only an observing and diagnosing science. The practical areas of bourgeois psychology are the professional selection, developed with the aid of the results of special investigations and mainly required because of the existence of an army of labor reserves in the capitalist countries; the reform of schools with the aid of "intelligence tests" for children; the development of methods of rationalization and labor training aimed exclusively at a radical exploitation of the working population; problems of the influence of advertising, etc. The educational psychology of bourgeois countries, especially in its consideration of problems of child psychology and pedagogy, starts from theoretical positions that are typical of paedology and deny the formative character of education. An education that corresponds to such conceptions is based only on the "natural" abilities of the children and influences merely the form of their expression.

The socialist practice of education is, on the other hand, the practice of an active and planned formation of human characteristics and abilities. The great aim set for our society—the transition to communism—means a substantial rise in the intellectual level of the whole working population. This is the task of our schools, and of our whole educational and cultural system. It is also

44

the task of our psychology. The consciousness of this task fundamentally changes our conception of psychology, of its connection with practice, of its concrete problems and methods.

Psychology changes from a registering science, which merely analyses the psychological processes and the peculiarities of personality, into a science of their mutability and transformation. From this point of view, the chief task of psychology is to study the processes through which science and ideology become the contents of human consciousness and deposit themselves in the psychological traits of personality.

The first requirement for the fulfillment of this task is a different conception of the connection between theory and practice. Psychology must start from the progressive experiences of education in our society; it must analyse these experiences and draw from them scientific generalizations on the child's psyche in connection with the general formative influence of the conditions of life, education and instruction. This is the only way to turn psychology into a science of the laws of the transformations of the mental factor which can fructify our practice in a progressive sense. The psychological development of man takes place through transformations which regularly appear in connection with the changes in his activities under the influence of new conditions and new tasks. This change in the activities and relationships of the child, the juvenile and the adult, is a process whose course is not evolutionary. It rather takes the form of sudden transformations. It is therefore no accident that the most progressive educational ideas—those of A. S. Makarenko—are ideas of a creative pedagogy, a "pedagogy of the events," which consciously and deliberately creates

45

educational opportunities.

This is also true of the process of teaching. To take an example: the child discovers, in his language classes, that the word, the language, are a peculiar reality—an object of knowledge and learning. Or else, in his mathematics classes, he achieves the transition to arithmetical fractions. These are *events* in the course of the child's school days, when he acquires the foundations of science.

How do these transformations and development thrusts take place? What are their "mechanisms" and the psychological laws that rule them? What measures prepare the process of development thrusts? What difficulties exist here?

The answers to these questions require that psychology acquire different methods. The abstract experiment, isolated from other methods of studying the laws of mental phenomena, is essentially an expression of a search for truth that is a stranger to reality and therefore cannot satisfy us. But we do not mean to imply by this that the method of experimental investigation, applied correctly and in its right place, should disappear from psychology. Rather, the importance of the experiment has become greater with regard to certain problems, though in a completely new form. In a certain sense it is the experiment of the pedagogical kind, although it serves to solve psychological problems. It requires a completely different organization of psychological investigation, which must be directly linked with practice and must undertake only the study of special questions. Such experiments should be undertaken jointly by psychologists and pedagogues. There exists a certain timidity in pedagogical and psychological circles about such psychological investigations of problems of practical work. This timidity is a symptom of the fear of responsibility. We are of the opinion that this attitude is contrary to the demand to change psychology from an abstract science into a living science, closely linked with practice. We believe that the intensification of the sense of responsibility for the education of our youth is a must for Soviet psychologists and the necessary precondition of a successful further development of Soviet psychology.

Notes

1. V. M. Borovski, *The Problem of the Instinct* (in Russian), in Reports of the Crimea Scientific Institute, vol. XI, pp. 99 f.

2. *Ibid.,* p. 104.

3. C. Darwin, *The Origin of Species.*

4. V. M. Borovski, *Historical and Critical Remarks on Reflexes and Instincts* (in Russian), 1946, p. 17.

5. S. L. Rubinstein, *General Foundations of Psychology* (in Russian), Moscow, 1945, pp. 32 f.

6. B. M. Teplov, "Abilities and Aptitude" (in Russian), in *Scientific Reports* of the Institute of Psychology, vol. XI, 1941. B. M. Teplov, *The Psychology of Musical Peculiarities* (in Russian), published by the Academy of the Pedagogical Sciences of the RSFSR, 1947.

7. W. Brown, *British Journal of Psychology,* 1944, p. 34.

8. K. N. Kornilov, "Psychology, Pedagogy and Educational Psychology" (in Russian), in *Soviet Pedagogy,* 1945, nr. 7, pp. 41 f.

HEREDITY AND THE
MATERIALIST THEORY

N. F. Posnanski

Bourgeois psychologists and pedagogues mostly emphasize the fatal influence of biological factors on man's developments and explain inborn characteristics through heredity. Human abilities are explained in theory as belonging to a specially formed aristocracy of birth and in practice as the privilege of the ruling classes and governors of colonies. Marxist theory, on the other hand, recognizes the individual differences between men, which appear at birth; but it does not see in inborn qualities any fatal predetermination of future talents and abilities that man develops in the course of his life. Individual differences between men are based on the existence of a definite physical organization and of particular natural life forces, which, according to Marx, are contained in man as tendencies and talents. Not everyone can be a Raphael, but only the person "in whom there is a Raphael" (Marx). This does not mean, of course, that everybody in whom there is a Raphael actually becomes a Raphael. The development of Raphaelian talents depends on the conditions of life and on education.

The inborn anatomic and physiological characteristics, as also the inborn type of nervous system, have much in common in all men at their birth. Individual differences express themselves but weakly in the vital function of individuals. Marx stated that "the original difference between a porter and a philosopher is less great than between a watch-dog and a greyhound. The gap between them exists through the division of labor."[1]

Individual talent, as long as it "does not begin to function as an actual force, exists only as a tendency."[2] The question here is to determine when it becomes active as an actual force. For the bourgeois idealist scientists and metaphysicians, it is from the very beginning an actual force, which directs the individual's development. The theory of dialectical materialism, however, excludes the existence of abilities before the appearance of the activity which first makes the ability effective. Ability is formed and develops only in the process of the activity that requires it. Marx noted that only music awakens the musical feeling in men. But to the idealists and metaphysicians, the role of the environment in developing abilities is reduced to the freeing of already existing ones. For the dialectical materialist, ability does not exist outside the corresponding activity of man. The tendencies from which it develops are too indefinite and plastic; they are too multivalent with regard to future development to be able to determine the character of future abilities.

Man is born with the tendency to speak. But if the child did not live in the society of men, but among animals, this tendency would not develop at all. Conditions of life and, above all, education, determine which language the child learns and the degree to which he learns it.

These facts lead to the conclusion that the concept "ability" has a historical character. The same applies to the connected concept of "talent." Human activity always takes place under concrete social and historical conditions. Different kinds of human activity are formed, change and disappear depending on their conditions; and so do human abilities. There can be no "philosophical talent" in a society that knows as yet no philosophy.

The feelings of men, too, change like their opinions, depending on their activities and their concrete historical living conditions.

Carlyle's chimera of "the animal nature of man burning in eternal hellfire," which tormented contemporary bourgeois pedagogues, does not exist for dialectical materialists.

But it is not only the abilities, talents and feelings of men that are historical in character: it is also their natural tendencies. It would be false to assume that these tendencies are the result of a purely biological heredity. In the course of man's history, and especially of the historical development of work, numerous differences in natural individual talents are bound to develop. The ever growing division of labor plays a decisive role in this process. As Marx puts it: "The differences in the natural talents of individuals are as much the cause as the effect of the division of labor."

In his critique of Stirner's view of the causes of the degeneration of individuals, Marx states that it had not occurred to Stirner to ponder these facts: that the child's capacity for development depended on the development of his parents; that the entire degeneration was created historically by the given circumstances and that it can be overcome by another historical development. Marx goes beyond this when he says that even naturally caused differences of birth, e.g. racial, can and must be abolished by a new historical development. This Marxian thesis disposes of all so-called race theories and of the political conclusions drawn from them. The conditions of life and work leave their imprint upon the individual's anatomic and physiological organisation and upon his nervous system. These results are to some degree passed on by heredity and consolidate in the descendants. Without such a heredity, there could have been no "humanization of the ape" or a further evolution of man. Pavlov's investigations showed that the acquisition of certain conditioned reflexes by animals facilitates the development of these same conditioned reflexes in the descendants of the animals experimented upon. Within the series of generations always subjected to the same experiment, the conditioned reflex gradually becomes an unconditioned reflex. This gives us a key to the understanding of the historical growth of the "hereditary differences." But, at the same time, it offers us the possibility of abolishing such differences.

Which factors among the individual's living and working conditions influence the development of his natural tendencies? The material means of production and the productive forces are the basic factors which determine the development of individual talents. Marx has thus analysed the factors which influenced the development of Raphael's pictorial talent: "Raphael, like any other artist, was conditioned by the technical advances of art that were made before his time; by the organisation of society and the division of labor in his locality; and finally, by the division of labor in all the countries with which his locality was in contact. It depends entirely on the demand for his work whether an individual like Raphael develops his talent; and this demand itself depends on the division of labor and the cultural conditions of men which develop from it."[3]

When we speak of the social conditions of the development of individual tendencies, we must emphasize one aspect of this process, i.e., the role of the collective. This is a difference of principle between dialectical materialism and the bourgeois theories, characterized by a pronounced individualism, viewed as a reflection of the economic competition. The bourgeois scientists develop their theories starting from the individual. Marx called these theories "Robinsonades."

A particularly good example of such theories in the field of education is Rousseau's "Emile." All kinds of "paedocentric" educational theories make their appearance until our day. It is above all Dewey's pedagogy, which likes to speak of the education of children in the "community." Dewey's view is best explained by his insistence that the child should become the center round which all the educational means turn. The Morgan-Mendel theory fully corresponds to his individualistic theory.

The dialectical materialist viewpoint, for which no individuals developing in isolation exist, stresses, on the contrary, the social conditioning of individuals. Marxism proves that man finds only in the community the possibilities for an all-sided development of his gifts.

In this connection, it must be pointed out that Marx and Engels distinguished between a true collectivity and a substitute form which only pretends to have a collective consciousness. Such a substitute is the bourgeois State, which offers freedom only to the individuals of the ruling class and only as long as they belong to this class.

The bourgeois pedagogues of imperialism who attempt to make the collective idea a reality in bourgeois schools through a pupils' self-government, a copy of the constitution of the bourgeois democratic State, create an apparent and substitute collectivity. Dewey's pedagogy, which wants to turn the school into "a cell of social, civic life," is a good example of an organisation of teaching and education founded on a substitute collective. The situation in a true collective is quite different. Of such a community Marx says: "It is a collective of revolutionary proletarians who take over the control over the conditions of their own existence and of all the other members of Society. In such a collectivity, individuals participate as individuals."[4] Such a true collectivity is the foundation of our Soviet system of education. It is not an accident but rather a historical necessity that the excellent educationist A. S. Makarenko should have appeared in the Soviet Union. He made "education by the collective for the collective" the motto of his pedagogical activity, and the excellent results which he achieved by his methods have, as Gorki emphasized, a world importance.

Notes

1. K. Marx and F. Engels, *Works* (in Russian), vol. V, p. 380.
2. *Ibid.*, vol. IV., p. 286.
3. K. Marx and F. Engels, *On Art and Literature* (in German), Berlin, 1950, p. 89.
4. K. Marx and F. Engels, *Works* (in Russian), vol. IV, p. 65.

THE INTELLECTUAL DEVELOPMENT OF THE CHILD

A. N. Leontiev

A. The Steps of the Child's Intellectual Development

It does not follow from the fact that education plays the decisive part in the child's intellectual development that education "can do everything" and that educators do not have to reckon with anything else. On the contrary, if they are to be successful in their educational and teaching work, they must always note *how* the development of the children takes place.

The intellectual and spiritual development of the child proceeds, like any other natural and social process, according to definite laws. This means that the development of the child proceeds consistently, from one stage of life to another. In this process, certain features of the childish psyche disappear, while others, qualitatively new, are formed. The educator must take this into account if he is to intervene actively in the process of formation of the growing personality.

There exist different periods or stages in the intellectual development of the child. The differences between them are not only quantitative but also qualitative. The intellectual development of the child is linked with a deep qualitative change in his personality. We can therefore speak of common psychological characteristics of children of certain ages: the pre-school child, the beginner at school, the adolescent. "He is a typical pre-school child" or "this is a typical adolescent" are phrases in common use. Though children of the same age differ from each other, they have many things in common in spite of their individual differences—provided that they live under the same social and historical conditions. It is this that causes the immediate impression that children of the same age look alike in certain respects.

The differences in the individual intellectual processes like memory, thought, etc. are both qualitative and quantitative. It is a well-known fact that smaller children learn verses by heart with considerably greater ease than do older ones. They can recite texts effortlessly and remember what they have learned for a long time. On the other hand, children of pre-school age cannot be expected to learn material of a length that pupils of higher classes manage without further ado. The explanation is not that the memory of a small child is simply better or worse than that of an older child, but rather that it is qualitatively different. What a small child easily memorizes may offer considerable difficulty to an older one, while, on the other hand, an adolescent may easily memorize something that is quite beyond the capacity of a young child. A four-year-old child that learned entire stories by heart and remembered them word by word, could not remember the names of the five fingers, i.e., five words.

He was able to memorize them only when his mother made them part of a game. It is well known that small children remember what they should learn most easily in playing. They cannot, as yet, set themselves the task of remembering this or that. They memorize easily only "what is remembered by itself." On the other hand, the memory of school children shows quite different qualitative characteristics. Children of that age group know how to remember deliberately what is required. It is therefore not true that the capacity of memorization simply increases with age; it is rather that memory changes qualitatively.

The same thing occurs in the development of other mental processes. The child's psyche therefore changes in the course of his development. The child of kindergarten age differs from the third-grade child in the character of his mental processes and in the special psychological traits peculiar to each stage of development.

In our country, learning at school starts at the age of seven. The most essential changes of the mental development occur precisely during the school age: memory is transformed, the way of thinking becomes different, the more complex forms of collective life and the sentiments pertaining thereto are formed, etc.

This particular example already shows that mental development is improved at every stage of life, while the child's psyche becomes more and more complex. It must be strongly emphasized in this connection that the content of these stages is not immutable or independent of the social conditions under which the child lives and grows. On the contrary, the content is determined by the concrete social and historical conditions; it is they that give this or that content to the child's life and activities. The process of the psychological development of the child is therefore essentially different under capitalism, which, in the words of Marx, robs the workers' children of their childhood, in contrast to our socialist order of society.

The conditions under which the Soviet children grow up are determined by the collective character of their society. They therefore escape such phenomena as self-doubt, loneliness, contrast between ideal and reality, which are characteristic of the life of children living under capitalism and which bourgeois psychology wrongly assumes to be universal.

The dependence of the stages of development of the child's psyche on the concrete historical conditions of life manifests itself also within the course of each stage. Even the general duration of the period of instruction and education, which is the period in which man is prepared for independent collaboration in social and economic life, has by no means always been the same. But it varied from era to era and was more extensive the higher were the requirements of society in each particular case. Also, in a society composed of antagonistic classes, it differed for children of different classes.

The stage of development is thus neither absolute nor predetermined; rather it is dependent on the concrete conditions of development and can change accordingly.

The following list of stages of the child's development is based on the study of the life and activity of children under the conditions of socialist society:

1) the stage of infancy, which includes the initial period of the child's life (up to the age of one);

2) the stage of early childhood (from 1 to 3 years);

3) the stage of the kindergarten age (from 3 to 6 years);

58

4) the stage of the early school age (from 7 to 10 years) ;

5) the stage of the middle school age (from 11 to 14 years) ; and

6) the stage of adolescence (from 14 to 17 years).

How does the transition from one stage to the next occur?

This transition could not take place if the child did not change in the course of the stage of development and thus prepare himself for the transition. Actually, the psychological and mental forces of the child develop more and more in the course of the activities typical of the given stage of development. Thus, during infancy, the activity of the child grows, and his perception and movement improve. His hands and feet become stronger and the cerebral cortex develops further. All this prepares the independent activity of the child and paves the way for an improved form of contact with the outside world, i.e., language.

The child's educator has the task of continuing his development on the basis of what has already been achieved. Above all, it is necessary to foster those characteristics of the child which prepare him for the next stage and which will therefore soon acquire a decisive importance in this connection. In other words, it is necessary to bear in mind not only the existing possibilities of the child but also the perspective of this further development. To do this, one must have a clear notion of the general course of the child's mental development.

It is not our purpose here to offer an extensive and exhaustive treatment of the way in which the child develops in the different stages and of the peculiar characteristics of these stages. We shall limit ourselves to con-

sidering some problems of development in the kindergarten and early school age.

B. *The Mental Development of Children in the Kindergarten Age*

At the threshold of the kindergarten age, i.e. towards
the end of the third and the beginning of the fourth year,
the child is generally accustomed to the objects in his
surroundings and has learned to use them correctly. He
knows how to handle the objects of daily use and likes
to play with all kinds of toys. He can already speak
fluently, listens with interest to short stories or verses,
looks at pictures, etc. A wide field of phenomena opens
itself to his eyes and ears. His activity is roused not only
by things that he encounters directly; under the influence
of earlier perceptions, he also feels the desire to do something, to undertake something. The child always thinks
up something else and tries to put his ideas into practice.
This is the time when the desire to do everything by
himself, so well known to the parents, becomes manifest.
"By myself" is the child's slogan, even when he still
needs the help of grownups so badly.

What is behind this form of the child's behavior? What
does it express?

A wide world of phenomena opens itself up to the
child at the beginning of the kindergarten age, and he
tries to grasp it. But a small child can grasp a phenomenon only concretely or "palpably." The child is
anything but a passive observer of these phenomena.
He wants to put into action through his own activities

60

everything that he has seen and that he has learned from the stories of grownups or from his children's books, even though so much cannot as yet be accessible to him. This is the ground on which contradictions arise between the diversity of the surrounding world that opens itself up to him and the limitations of his actual possibilities of action. The new things that the child discovers in the world around him are, above all, kinds of human activity and men's attitudes towards things. The book, the exercise book, etc., are the things with which his elder brother, the pupil, has to do; the gun and the cannon are the sphere of activity of the soldier. The child sees all these things but it is forbidden to him to touch them and to handle them. He does not as yet possess the necessary skills.

How are these contradictions resolved? The way in which the children get over them is a new kind of activity making its appearance at that time: the creative playing of parts. This does not take place in the play of the earlier childhood. What matters to the child in this new kind of play is to act as exactly as possible the way his father or his brother, a chauffeur or an officer acts, i.e., to take over and play a certain part. In this play, the children become familiar, through creative activity, with certain events that take place in their surroundings: a railway trip, the visit of a doctor, the building of a factory. It might seem, at first glance, that such games lead the child out of the real world and into the world of fantasy and imagination. But it is not so. Let us take, as an example, children playing at "war." Everything here seems to be an illusion: a simple stick serves as a "rifle," little Peter suddenly becomes "Sergeant" and Vania "Major" and all this is but "make believe." But not quite. Such a game does not require the actual objects involved; nor is it a question of carrying out the actions exactly. What matters to the child is that reality is correctly reflected in the contest of the actions of the game and in the relations thus created. If the game involves shooting, it can, of course, only be a make-believe shooting. But, on the other hand, since the real soldier must not desert his post and the real sergeant must not give orders to the real major—such things must also not happen in the game.

The creative play with distributed parts is an activity most important for the mental development of the child of pre-school age (3 to 5 years). Not only the child's imagination and fantasy are developed in it, but also his mental capacities. The play forms his personality, his collective spirit. "The play," said Gorki, "is at the same time a way by which the children learn to know the world in which they live and which they are called upon to change."

The creative play of pre-school age children must not be viewed as meaningless pastime and unimportant for the child's development. Rather, the best attempt must be made to direct this play and to enrich it. N. K. Krupskaya writes on children's games: "Even if the train in which they travel is made of chairs, and the house they build is made of bits and pieces, the child learns during play to overcome obstacles, to know the world around him and to deal with such difficulties as may arise."[1]

When stimulating the children to educationally valuable games, it must be seen to that they receive useful impressions and suggestions. This does not mean, of course, that everything which the child takes from his surroundings becomes part of his play and is accepted among his conceptions. It is sometimes necessary to divert the children from the play theme they had chosen into another, more desirable one. This can be easily done if the child knows that the grownups follow his play with interest and sympathy.

It is good when the children play in the presence of grownups. A few words can achieve much in such a case, for the activity of the child in creative play can easily be diverted into the direction desired.

Creative play is, as a rule, collective. As the roles are distributed, certain definite relations are created between the children which condition their behavior towards each other. The accepted role determines the child's behavior. "The daughter" must obey "the mother"; "the mother" must be loving; "the policeman" strict but courteous. We must not forget that the main thing for the children in these games is action and, in particular, an action which comes closest to reality. The children always take seriously the content of the actions performed in the play. Therefore, a remark thrown in incidentally is sufficient to direct the behavior of the playing child. It is enough to say, for example: "Does it really happen that a policeman on duty is uncourteous?", and the quarrel among the playing children subsides. The play is a kind of school in which the child acquires creatively the rules and forms of human behavior and of the reciprocal relations between men. The play of our Soviet children becomes, therefore, a school in which they practically acquire the norms of Socialist behavior. But, to make creative play truly fruitful, it is necessary to overcome the prejudice that play is a "free" activity which tolerates no intervention from adults. We must

not shy from conducting and directing the play by relying on its characteristic peculiarities. In creative play,
the objects which the children have to use may be fiction, e.g., the stick instead of the rifle, the chair instead
of the car. The movements of the playing may also be
fiction, e.g., imitations of the actual motions that the
hand performs in shooting, instead of the real thing.
But the contents of these actions and the relations between the people concerned are not fictions, for the
child always strives after truth and reality. He always
likes to listen to grownups explaining to him how this
or that action "actually takes place in reality." This is
what we can rely on when we direct their play and
educate them in the process.

The notes of a Moscow teacher, S. A. Cherepanova,
are quoted below as an example of how children's games
are directed:

"Igor and the other boys have built a big bus from
chairs, while the girls play with dolls. I suggest to Igor
to invite the girls to a bus trip. 'I am the conductor, I
punch the passengers' tickets,' says Galia. 'No, I want
to be the conductor,' answers Vania. A quarrel breaks
out. Vova argues with Igor about who is to be the
driver. 'You were driving before; now it is my turn,'
he says. The teacher must now intervene. I explain to
the children that both driver and conductor have their
shifts, and that one rests while the other works. The
children like the idea of my trying to turn their play
into the 'real thing.' 'Is this what always happens with
real drivers?' asks Vova. Peace is restored. Igor passes
the steering wheel to the boy who relieves him, while
Vania waits until he can relieve Galia, now acting as
conductor."

64

Creative play forms many psychic processes of children of pre-school age, especially in the early and middle period. This is proved by the results of Soviet investigations. Thus, a study of the memory of 4 to 6 year olds showed that the number of words memorized in creative play is double the number memorized at the order of adults. The same is true of the child's ability to control his movements; this is especially important for the future, i.e., for the school years. Investigations of Soviet psychologists proved that normal time during which children are able to pay attention to the position of their upper body, hands and feet and to maintain them in a given position is 40 seconds. But in a game in which the children play at "positions" this time increases more than sixfold.

These examples show clearly why play must be given a great educational significance in pre-school age. The outstanding Soviet educationist, A. S. Makarenko, wrote: "In the education of the future personality, the play must by no means be abolished; it must rather be organized in such a way that, while remaining play, it nevertheless develops the qualities of the future worker and citizen."[2]

It must not, however, be assumed that the entire development of the child of pre-school age occurs in creative play. The play is but *one* of the ways in which the child comes to know the surrounding world.

Introduction to culture is another important way to the child's mental and moral development. A. S. Makarenko rightly maintained that cultural education must begin as early as possible—before the child knows how to read and write, as soon as he is able to see, hear and speak properly.

The cultivation of a proper attitude towards books is a matter of urgent necessity in this connection. We must not believe that the child's attitude to books is something that forms only at school, when he has learned to read independently. Rather, it develops at the earliest age. When the child sees that the grownup members of his family read books attentively, when he realizes that books play an important part in their lives, he acquires a respect for books. When the child looks at pictures and listens to stories and tales, he not only enriches his mental outlook, but also becomes interested in books. This interest prepares him to learn reading and writing. Even the newspaper, which the grownups constantly use to keep informed about events in the outside world, no doubt plays a certain part in the early impressions of the child.

Even more important for the development of the child are such things as his practical activities, the demands made upon him by the grownups, and his position in the family. These things determine the development of the psychological qualities of his personality which will be all-important for his future work and life in the collective.

Negative traits of character such as egoism or callousness are caused both by a defective education for work and by an insufficiently developed sense of collectivity. An exhaustive investigation of these problems would go beyond the limits of our study of the mental and psychological development of the child. These are special pedagogical problems. We will limit ourselves to pointing out the most important conditions of an adequate education of the child in this respect.

One of the most important of these conditions is that

the child becomes familiar, from the very beginning, with the work of his parents and other members of his family. "The child must learn, as soon as possible, where his father or mother works, the kind of work they do, whether it is heavy, what kind of effort it requires and what achievements it brings. He must know that his father or mother are engaged in productive work and must realize the importance that their production has for the whole of society. . . . The child must understand, as soon as possible, that the money that his parents bring home is not merely a useful thing to spend, but the reward for a great and socially useful work. The parents must always find both time and simple words to explain this to the child. If the mother does not work outside, but at home, the child must also come to know and respect her kind of work; he must understand that it, too, requires effort and strain."[3]

The second important condition is that the child acquire certain working skills already at the kindergarten age. The child should gradually be given certain simple but continuous tasks, such as, to water flowers, to feed the cat, to clear up his own things and toys, to take the incoming newspaper to a certain place every day, etc.

Our socialist society produced the Soviet family, the germ cell of our society, pervaded by the collective spirit. This has created quite new conditions for the family education. It is most important that this favorable opportunity should be made use of fully. The child must not be alienated from family life; he must rather be led to this life, so that he can feel himself to be a member of the family collective.

C. The Early School-Age Child

When the parents are asked what they believe to be the
most important thing in the development of their school-
age children, they generally answer: "How he learns at
school." We must, of course, agree with this answer. It
is therefore very understandable that many parents pay,
as a rule, so much attention to the successes of their children at school. But all parents do not realize—far from
it—that the performance of their children at school
depends, especially at the beginning, on the way in which
the child has been prepared for his attendance at school.
Many parents seem not to understand fully the very question of the degree of the preparation of their children
for school attendance. But this question must be treated
with the utmost seriousness. The successes and failures of
the child at school depend on it.

What do we mean when we talk of "the child's readiness
for school"?

Instruction at school makes, from the very first days, a
series of demands on the child. When he enters school he
must already possess a certain knowledge and some simple
skills. The more of this knowledge and skills he has, the
better he is prepared. The preparation must, of course,
come as early as possible. Great attention is paid to this
preparation in our kindergartens. There, the children
are subjected to organized activities which are to prepare
them for attendance at school. But the child must also be
prepared for school in his family circle, as regards his
general mental development.

From his very first days at school the child must learn
how to listen to the teacher actively and without letting

68

himself be distracted. He must memorize what he is asked to remember and not what he is interested in, and he therefore remembers, so to say, automatically. It is no less important that he pay attention to his behavior. He must be able to sit still at his desk, and to get up from it together with the other pupils of his class. But the most important thing of all is that the child be educated into a proper attitude towards school attendance and given a proper understanding of the importance of education.

The child's going to school is an extraordinary milestone in the course of his life. By going to school, the child enters upon a new stage of his development which gives his life a new content. The child consciously acquires at school a new position in human society, i.e., the rank of a Soviet schoolchild. Learning becomes for him an obligatory and social activity which is determined by law. The quality of his learning activity becomes the subject of an objective social evaluation; it determines from now on the attitude of the environment to the child. His performance gives him a definite rank in his collective, e.g. he may become a model pupil.

Together with new duties, the pupil acquires new rights. Thus, he has from now on the right to expect that grown-ups bear his school tasks in mind and do not disturb him at his homework.

A beginner at school must be prepared not only for a systematic acquisition of knowledge, but also for the new social relationships which are formed at school.

It is a well-known fact that children of pre-school age are eager to go to school. This desire for school is a necessary and important condition of readiness for school. When the child becomes a pupil, he enters upon a new life, starts upon an activity whose importance is recognized by all. Everybody takes school seriously, even the newspapers and radio publish reports about it. This desire for school must be fostered, for it is the foundation for the most important thing of all: a proper, conscious and responsible attitude of children towards their school as a whole.

Soviet school children are generally respected. It is therefore necessary that the child encounter within his family such respect for his school, for his teacher and for the dignity of a Soviet pupil.

It is also important to form in the child a proper attitude towards his learning activity. Learning requires from him the capacity to achieve a definite result. The child must not merely dispose of the homework in a perfunctory manner. He must really "learn" it, i.e get to know it thoroughly and not superficially. The child must therefore learn to estimate the results of his learning activity correctly. Already the kindergarten pupils of the later age groups must be educated to strive consistently for the achievement of a definite purpose and to finish what they have started, even if it is of minor importance. The performance of the child must be carefully watched. His achievements must be given recognition, and even his smallest successes must not meet with indifference.

Learning at school requires systematic work from the child. A pupil who is not used to work will never be able to learn properly. As we said above, the capacity for consecutive effort and the proper attitude to work must be developed in the child already at the kindergarten stage.

The experience gathered in our schools shows that the children who had to carry out certain definite if small tasks at home before they entered school learn more rapidly than others how to organize their schoolwork properly.

70

These are the chief elements in the development of the child's personality during the preparation for his attendance at elementary school.

The importance of the school for the mental development of the child is extraordinarily great. If we consider more closely the changes in the child's mental processes in his school years, we find that all these changes take place under the influence of the systematic instruction received at school.

From his very first year at school the child gradually develops the ability to listen to the teacher's explanation with ever greater endurance and concentration. This means that the child's attention becomes more and more constant.

Memory improves more and more under the influence of the teacher's instruction. The child memorizes educational material and learns many things by heart. His memory increasingly acquires a clear and logical character.

Particularly pronounced is the development of the child's thinking in the school years. In the lower grades, thinking is still rather concrete and bound up with pictorial representation. At this age, the child's thought still sticks largely to facts and ideas that can be vividly illustrated. What the child has actually seen and heard plays an important part in his thought.

The child learns at school to make correct generalizations even about relatively complex phenomena; but these generalizations are not yet precise or systematic enough. By acquiring knowledge systematically, the child learns to think consistently, i.e. to bind individual phenomena into logical connections.

The mother tongue is of great importance for the mental development of the younger school children. By learning his mother tongue, the child not only acquires the ability to read and to write—things important in themselves for his mental development—but also consciously develops a proper form of expression.

Our Soviet school does not limit itself to transmitting knowledge to the child and developing his mental processes. It also educates him and forms his personality, the personality of a Soviet patriot and of a future fighter for Communism. The school also opens up for the child those wide perspectives that await him in our Socialist society.

We all know the great successes of our school. The heroic deeds of its pupils in work and battle are known the world over. But our school is not alone in its activity. In its work it has the support of the Soviet family and of our entire community. In educating the child, the school works hand in hand with the family. It is therefore inadmissible for parents to say that they "need not bother any more" about the mental development of their child and the formation of his personality, "because the school is taking care of all that." Successful instruction, good education and a proper course of the child's development all presuppose tireless effort on the part of the parents.

We have already mentioned the importance of a proper attitude on the part of the child towards his school and his duty to learn, even before he begins to attend school. The importance of this attitude becomes even greater once the child is at school. A new task arises here for the teacher: to put this sense of duty upon firm foundations and to strengthen it—for a full development of the pupil's personality is impossible without it. This sense of duty must be fostered from the very beginning of school. Its absence will produce very deleterious effects

72

in the future and will lead to the growth of most undesirable character traits. How is the proper attitude towards school and its duties consolidated in the child? Above all, by an attentive and understanding behavior of the grown-ups towards the child's learning activity. They must always speak of instruction at school with respect and approval, and must always rouse the child's interest in his schoolwork. From the very beginning of his school attendance, the child must be urged to do his schoolwork according to plan. Above all, a certain definite time period is to be fixed in which the child must do his daily homework. The child must also be helped to prepare a working plan to provide for the performance of his homework and for the necessary periods of leisure.

At the beginning, it is very important to urge the child to be careful in his schoolwork and to exercise a certain self-control. After all, the little pupil does not yet know how to work properly and how to do his homework: he often keeps his books and exercise-books in disorder, not because he is disorderly by nature but only because he simply does not know yet how to handle such things. The same applies to his self-control. It sometimes seems to him that he has done his homework thoroughly. But this may not actually be the case: he may have "overlooked" this or that, and the homework is not at all "done." The child has not checked this—sometimes he is altogether unable to do the checking.

It is at home that the child must consolidate the ability to learn which he has acquired at school. This is why parents must always show interest in what the teacher requires in this respect. Their interest not only helps the child to remember the teacher's instructions in time and to follow them; it also accustoms him to the idea that these instructions are something that grownups take seriously and respect.

But sometimes the interest of grownups in the child's homework turns into a wrong and inappropriate form of help. Some parents, when supervising the homework and making the child do it, tell him what to do and how to do it—they even solve the problems for him! A teacher reported in the magazine "Family and School" that "a mother, to ease her son's homework, used to read aloud the oral assignment, which the boy merely had to repeat. We also know another mother who solves the problems with the pupil: she reads the assignment and formulates the questions—while the pupil writes the answers in the exercise books without mistakes and without inkblots!"

And here is another example of wrongly understood "help." Nina, a third-grade pupil, sits at home doing her homework. The mother does some other work in the same room. From time to time, Nina asks a question. For example: " 'How much is seven times eight?' 'Fifty-six', answers the mother mechanically, and thinks she has done a good deed and has helped her daughter with her homework."

Although Nina is already able to solve such problems by herself, she is used to help, even if she does not need it. Such "help" cannot be justified: it produces no positive results, only negative ones. If the homework is taken from the child, he becomes irresponsible and gets used to relying on others instead of on himself.

It is, of course, necessary to help the pupil if need be, to take interest in him and to keep a check on how he does his homework. But one should not impair the independence of his work or take away his responsibility for it. On the contrary, his independence and his sense of responsibility must be fostered by all possible means.

If the child is to maintain a serious and correct attitude toward his education, he must be aware that his parents, too, respect his school and his teacher. We cannot expect a child to have respect for his school and for the authority of his teacher if his family is wanting in such respect. Such things happen, alas. "Komsomolskaya Pravda" reports the case of a woman teacher who asked the mother of a bad pupil to come to her for a talk. She received the following answer from the girl herself: "Mother says, if you need her, you can come to her."

One cannot help feeling indignant over such things. Such an attitude not only undermines the proper attitude of the child towards his school and his teacher; it often also hurts the child's feelings and injures him. The principal of a Moscow school reports: "When Mira heard her father, who was looking over her exercise book, make a negative remark about her teacher, she cried and said, in tears, that she would never again show her exercise books to anybody."

The development of the child's personality in elementary school consists not only of the extension of his knowledge, the cultivation of his thinking and similar mental processes, but also of the formation of a conscious, responsible attitude to his duties, of his education in a sense of duty. But this is only possible if the pupil respects his school. This feeling of respect for the school is the first step in developing a consciousness that to learn well is "the greatest patriotic deed of a Soviet child," in the words of M. I. Kalinin.

It is wrong to assume that the younger pupil cannot achieve the consciousness of the social importance of his learning activity. Learning at school offers the possibility to satisfy the child's awakening desire for a new rank in life. This new rank includes for the child the consciousness that he has become a learner, a pupil. His attitude towards education must therefore be correctly developed in the days to follow.

Other essential changes that are characteristic for this stage of development are the formation of a conscious discipline, and the development of the capacity for systematic work. These are the first and most important steps in the development of the child's will. The family also plays an important part in the formation of this characteristic of the child's personality.

To form the child's will, he must be urged to get used, unerringly and without deviation, to a certain order, which should include the performance of certain domestic duties. This order has an immense importance in the child's life. When the child is, for any reason, withdrawn from his accustomed order and lives "in freedom," his general condition worsens, he becomes dissatisfied and irritable.

Finally, we must emphasize another important change in the child's psyche which occurs during the school years.

The very entrance into school, i.e., into a collective, places the child in conditions which give him a powerful impulse towards the development of the collective spirit and of the common care for good learning. His collaboration in the social organization of children is also essential for the development of these collective traits of character. The parents act very correctly when they permit and encourage their child to take part in the work of the "Pioneers" (i.e., Soviet Boy and Girl

76

Scouts). The following incident is interesting in this connection.

The girl L. was asked by a group of pioneers to take part in a sporting event so that she could defend her title as best sportswoman. But the girl refused on the ground that she was to go to the theater that day. She was urged, she was told that a theater ticket would be available for her for another day, but she persisted in her refusal. The parents found out about this, came to the Pioneers' meeting, and criticized their daughter's behavior. This made a great impression not only on the girl herself, but on the others as well. On the other hand, the attitude of parents who underestimate the participation of their children in the social organizations of children is wrong. It happens that even an event as important in the child's life as his entrance into the Pioneers organization is not given its due importance in the family, is not discussed, and does not become the occasion for a family celebration that the child remembers for many years.

The parents do not always show sufficient interest in the child's activities in the Pioneers, which is likely to spoil the child's joy in these activities.

The mental development of the child is by no means a process which takes place independently of education. On the contrary, the development of all the child's relations with life and reality, of his entire activity and consciousness, is determined in its course by education. At the different stages of the child's development, it is now one relation to reality and now another, now one kind of activity and now another, that plays an important part. But whatever stage of development we might consider, we will find that not only the kindergarten and the school, but also the family, plays a significant role in the formation of the child's personality.

We address the parents with the words of F. E. Dzierzhinsky:

"You are faced with an immense task: to educate and to form your children. Be on guard! For the parents bear a high measure of responsibility not only for the qualities of their children, but also for their defects."[4]

Notes

1. N. K. Krupskaya, *The Role of Play in the Kindergarten* (in Russian), Pedagogical Publishing House, 1948, p. 5.

2. A. S. Makarenko, *Lectures on the Education of Children,* Volk und Wissen Verlag, Berlin/Leipzig, 1949, p. 37.

3. A. S. Makarenko, *Lectures on the Education of Children* (in Russian), p. 84.

4. From *Soviet Pedagogy,* Nr. 11/12, 1941, p. 56.

PROBLEMS OF THE CHILD'S PERSONALITY FORMATION

G. S. Kostiuk

The Soviet psychologists, armed with the theory of dialectical materialism, have set about creating a theory of the growing personality. Soviet psychology has generalized from the experience gathered in the education of the younger generation of our people in the spirit of communism and the successful formation of the consciousness of adults in the process of Socialist construction. It is based on the investigation of questions of the psychology of education, instruction and development, and on the scientific results of the related sciences. It also makes use of everything valuable developed by the great thinkers of the past. Soviet psychology has therefore already achieved some remarkable results which compare favorably with fatalistic Western psychology.

Lenin wrote: "Everybody in the twentieth century—or even at the end of the nineteenth century—agrees with 'the principle of development.' Yes, but the superficial, thoughtless, accidental, philistine 'agreement' is an agreement of a kind that stifles and blots out truth."[1] The agreement with the principle of development reached by the bourgeois child psychology, born at the end of the nineteenth century, an age of sharpened class war, was such a means of stifling and trivializing truth.

Preyer, whom the bourgeois historians of psychology present as the founder of child psychology, offers a clear and unambiguous formulation of the aims of that branch of psychology in the introduction to his book "The Soul of the Child." He writes there: "It must, above all, be clear that the basic functions which emerge after birth, are not formed only after birth. If they did not exist before birth, it would be impossible to determine where they come from." Therefore, "some parts of the ovum content must undoubtedly possess potential mental capacity." This human capacity is not therefore "formed anew every time from material incapable of sensitivity, but is differentiated in ovum parts as their hereditary characteristic." In other words, "the soul of the child is not a tabula rasa"; rather, it is inscribed "with many illegible, irrecognizable and invisible signs." He sees the task of his book, and the job of child psychology in general, to note and illuminate these signs so as "to recognize and decipher the secret writing in the soul of the child." [2]

Thus Preyer formulated—ninety years after the Russian radical Radishchev and over forty years after the Russian critic Belinsky wrote on the same topic—his conception of the child's psyche, which is often idealistic and is hostile to the true principle of development. His theory shaped the character of most Western studies of child psychology at the end of the nineteenth and the beginning of the twentieth century.

It is no accident that this branch of psychology was

80

formed contemporaneously with the pedagogical theories of Stanley Hall, Kilpatrick, and others, and with the theories of heredity of Weismann and Mendel. The motivation for these theories lies, as our great Darwinist K. A. Timiryazev pointed out, in the wish of the reactionary forces to stop the progress of the materialistic conception of life; in the revived clerical reaction against Darwinism; and in the flare-up of a narrow-minded German nationalism. As he put it: "The future historian of science will regretfully note the penetration of clerical and nationalist elements in the brightest sphere of human activity, which aims at uncovering the truth and protecting it from all abuse."[3]

According to these conceptions, the development of living organisms is reduced to a simple repetition and regeneration of those characters and properties which are allegedly contained from the start in some hereditary mass that is autonomous, independent of the organism, uninterrupted and imperishable. Nothing new is formed in this process. These conceptions, under cover of phrases about evolution, essentially deny true evolution and restore the idealistic ideas of preformism, which had long ago been abandoned. As Timiryazev put it: "This makes it understandable why they were taken over with such glee by the enemies of all theories of evolution, and why anti-Darwinists and parsons joyfully embraced Mendelism and soon created a whole school, whose 'blissful' field of action was open to everyone. For no knowledge or capacity was required, not even the ability to think logically."[4]

It is also understandable why these reactionary Weismann-Mendel-Morgan conceptions of heredity, which are hardly ever applied in the practice of bourgeois agriculture, were so widely applied to man and why, in so many reports on investigations and lectures on child psychology by men like Claparède, Bühler, Thorndike, etc., the results of experiments with sweetpeas and fruit flies were so widely applied to human heredity. These authors wanted to find a theoretical justification for their obsolete metaphysical theories of human personality. By proclaiming the immutability of man's psychic qualities, they tried and still try to prove the eternal character of capitalist conditions and to justify racism, cosmopolitanism, etc.

We can justify this assertion by some examples. Thus K. Bühler, whose idealistic conception of the child's psychic development aims at proving how, in general, "the spirit (Geist) becomes what it essentially (an sich) is," makes an extensive use of the Weismann-Mendel theory of heredity for his proofs. He not only asserts that this theory has allegedly directed the study of human heredity into a "certain definite path that is rich in prospects," but tries to apply it directly to the study of the growth of mental characteristics, of individual differences and even of the peculiarities of moral behavior. He explains the differences in moral behavior not by the unfavorable conditions of capitalist society that drive men into committing crimes, but by heredity. He writes: "There are men who have from their youth an indestructible desire to be thieves and tramps, and who become in later life regularly returning guests of prisons and penitentiaries. They possess a fatal inheritance which is transmitted from generation to generation with the same regularity as any simple bodily characteristic. . . . But it must be borne in mind that this tendency makes these men commit acts that lead to terms in prisons and penitentiaries only so often as is required by the Mendelian laws."[5]

Other authors reach the same conclusions. E. Huguenin ignores the very statistical material which she quotes in her study and which proves the frequency of juvenile delinquency in bourgeois society, when she asserts in her study that the causes of this delinquency lie in "pathological hereditary tendencies" and "hereditary degenerations" which "explain the anomalies of reason, of will and of emotion." She goes on to say that: "The biological study of the juvenile delinquent proves that he is almost always the victim of a difficult heredity and that he is burdened with physical and mental defects inherited from his forebears."[6]

The Weismann-Mendel-Morgan conceptions of heredity have completely pervaded several trends of contemporary bourgeois psychology. The literature that is published in the United States provides ample proof of this assertion. Thus, Thorndike, in his theory of development, attributes a decisive influence to heredity. In his opinion, human nature or the human type is "a certain definite collection or battery of genes which work together in a thousand different ways and means." This "supply of genes does not change from generation to generation and remains the same, independently of conditions of life." It allegedly determines not only physical traits, the shape of the face, the color of the eyes or skin, but also the mental traits of man. Thorndike attempts to present a detailed picture of how these "genes of consciousness" determine in children their "ability to move from the spot, to run, to jump, to embrace, to fight, to pursue, to cry, to laugh, to study with hands and eyes, to perform a constructive or destructive ac-

83

tion," and also reason, the ability to speak and to learn, different professional capacities and psychological qualities. Thorndike, like the other American representatives of the "two-factor" theory which is so widely held in that country, does not deny the importance of the environment in the development of the child. But he insists that the decisive part in this process, and in the differences observed in it, is played by "the battery of genes" of each individual which determine his inborn abilities and his "membership in the white and not in the colored race."[7]

Other American scientists who investigate human abilities with the aid of the famous aptitude tests, develop similar racist views. They try to camouflage their primitive and unscientific methods with the aid of complicated apparatus and scientific formulas. Their intention is to prove that the development of abilities in children is determined not by the social conditions of life but by the inherited biological equipment, the gene; that the abilities do not develop with age but "remain constant with regard to age"; and that the children of colored peoples are far behind the children of white peoples as far as their abilities are concerned. This difference can allegedly not be wiped out by their adhesion to the white man's civilization.

It must be noted in this connection that a number of the other American writers have reached similar reactionary conclusions from, so to say, opposite starting points. They ascribe the decisive part to the environment, but hold it to be immutable. They view it as a purely external environment and limit it to the influence of food, climate and the geographical factor. Their argument may be different, but their purpose is

84

the same: it is an attempt to prove the physical and psychological inferiority of the workers and the so-called lower races and to justify the right of Anglo-American imperialism to exploit them in an inhuman fashion.

Bourgeois psychology has entered, in its main tendencies, into the service of capitalist imperialism. It is therefore unable to solve the problem of personality and other psychological problems. From this arises its complete renunciation of the principle of development. Bourgeois psychologists try to explain the concrete historical peculiarities of man, which were formed by the material living conditions of society, as eternal and immutable characteristics of "man in general." They try to find the driving forces of man's development in "the depths of biological drives" and to explain man's degeneration under capitalism by references to "human nature."

This also explains the attempts to provide a psychological justification of the different philosophical systems and ideas that are still used by the enemies of Marxism in spite of their untenable character. This was noted by Zhdanov, who said that these were, above all, ". . . Neo-Kantianism, theology, the old and new editions of agnosticism, and the attempts to smuggle God and other kinds of nonsense into modern natural science, which are used to renew the stock-in-trade of the idealistic shopkeepers." [8]

The crisis of modern bourgeois psychology is acknowledged by the representatives of progressive psychology in the West. Some of them rightly admit that modern psychology in capitalist countries "is in the service of the ruling class"; that "the hierarchy of its problems is determined by the interests of that class"; that the

85

theses of that psychology are "merely the projections of bourgeois morality"; that "child psychology, for example, was formed on the assumption that only bourgeois children existed in this world"; and that bourgeois psychologists, and the psychotechnicians in particular, try "to ignore the class struggle" and "to float above it" by applying the comparative method while they actually serve the needs of capitalism and rationalize the exploitation of the workers."[9]

They correctly state the reasons for this crisis of bourgeois psychology: "Bourgeois psychology is idealist, while it should be materialist"; "psychology can become a science only if it renounces idealism, but the psychologists of today are unable to renounce it"—which is understandable, since "they are linked with it by their origin, tradition and bourgeois ideology." In the best of cases, "they base themselves on the imperfect forms of materialism which prove to be sterile," i.e., on physiological and mechanistic materialism. More often, they "busy themselves altogether too much with restoration of spiritualism and scholasticism." Although they "abandoned the monk's cowl and have put on the lay clothing of professors," they "remain essentially theologians." Their psychology is "a chapter of theology and an instrument of the state." Instead of spreading knowledge, "they offer to the masses Bergsonian mystifications, the fog of German metaphysical psychology, or the kind of psychological cocktail that is mixed by psychoanalysis."[10]

The author cited above notes that a Catholic periodical "described his criticism of the foundations of psychology as the undertaking of a Bolshevik." He is convinced that psychology will become a genuine science only after it attacks all its problems in a new way, puts

86

an end to idealism, and accepts "the point of view of modern materialism, originated by Marx and Engels and called dialectical materialism." Only this materialism can "be the correct ideological basis of a positive psychology."[11]

*　　*

*

The education of children at school is a common activity of the children and of the teacher which takes place in the school collective. It therefore requires from the children a certain attitude not only towards education but also towards the collective, an observance of the rules of behavior at school and in society. The school collective and also the collectives of the Pioneer and Young Communist (Komsomol) organizations represent necessary assumptions for the formation of the growing personality; for the individual "receives only in the collective the means which make it possible for him to develop his gifts all-sidedly. Personal freedom is therefore possible only in the collective."[12]

This is an important principle of Soviet education; it has been excellently realized especially in the educational theory and practice of A. S. Makarenko. Makarenko shows that the creation of a sound collective, the purposes and strivings of which are inseparably linked with the life of our society constitutes a necessary precondition and powerful force for the full development of the personality of every child; for the removal of negative character traits; for the formation of his attitudes, his will, and his character; and for the development of his abilities. It was by his able realiza-

87

tion of the principle of education in the collective, by the collective and for the collective that Makarenko turned so many young people damaged by life whom the professional educationists proclaimed hopeless and "biologically doomed," into full and active workers for Socialist construction. One important feature of that education is that it is realized not only by the conscious activity of grownups, but that it also relies on the unfolding and ever more conscious activity of the child himself. For the child is never just a passive object of the influence of environment and education. As Makarenko puts it, "We must free ourselves from the great 'vice of pedagogy,' i.e., from the belief that the children are the objects of education. No, they are the living life, and a very beautiful life at that. . . ."

The things which surround the child influence him by entering somehow into his life and becoming the objects and conditions of his activity. When the child acts, he changes the influence of his surroundings. The activity, controlled by education, not only satisfies his needs, desires and strivings, but also establishes new motives and aims for new activities and skills through which these objectives are reached. The change in the internal conditions of development in the child brings about changes in his demands on his surroundings and in the influence of his surroundings upon him. That which up to now has not existed for the child and has had no influence on him, now begins to affect him. Not only the family, the kindergarten or the school, but also the events of the social and political life of our country gradually become, through changes in the child, preconditions of his further psychological development. The growing consciousness and self-consciousness of the child is here the important factor, without which the ever more complex reciprocal relations of the child and his surroundings cannot be understood. The child's consciousness is, indeed, an ideal form in which his life expresses itself, but it also becomes a real factor which affects his life. Lenin wrote: "The concept of the transformation of the ideal into the real is a deep one and very important for history. But it is also clear from man's personal life that there is much truth in it."[13]

The individual characteristics of the child also express themselves in his reciprocal relations with his surroundings. He is attracted by some things and the activities connected with them; he is enthusiastic about them and imitates them knowingly or unknowingly. He is indifferent to other things, avoids them or even acts against them. Depending on such attitudes, the roles of the various environmental conditions on the child's mental development also differ. On the other hand, all attempts to establish a direct dependence between certain personality traits of the child and some definite "environmental factors" are false. The real reciprocal relations that develop in the environment and become important in real life must be borne in mind; but neither can we ignore the great role of education which leads and directs these reciprocal relations.

It is clear from the above why we must definitely overcome not only the idealistic but also the mechanistic views on the psychological development of the child. These views, widely popular in contemporary psychology, especially among the Americans (Watson, etc.), destroy the possibilities that actually exist for the development and education of children by asserting that this development is some kind of internal process which only receives its impulse from some external influences of the environment. Such psychologists rob these processes of their rich content and confuse the educators in their practical work. The remnants of such views have not yet been liquidated in our scientific literature and practice. They make themselves felt in the statements of some physiologists who have not yet given up hope of referring all psychological development to physiological factors. They can also be found, in part, in the work of some pedagogues who do not feel inclined to stimulate a conscious activity among the children or who try to shift responsibility for the negative character traits of some of their pupils and their failures at school by blaming their unfavorable living conditions.

The recognition of the social conditioning of the psychological development of the child by no means releases us from the task assigned to us by Lenin, i.e., to understand this process of development as a "spontaneous movement with an inner necessity."

Since we reject the idealistic concept of spontaneity, which underlies the thought of so many bourgeois psychologists, we must explain it in a dialectical materialist fashion.

The spontaneity of the child's psychological development is not in contradiction with the conditioning of this development by society; rather, it derives from it. The new needs, strivings and interests of the child and other stimuli of his activity do not come from some intrinsic "nature" of the child, distinct from the world around him. They grow out of his life, which is inseparably linked with the life of his society and is directed by education. This is proved both by our entire pedagogical practice and by the results of investigations of Soviet psychologists like A. N. Leontiev, A. A. Smirnov, etc. These investigations reveal how the aims and motives of the child's activities are formed; and show the qualitative peculiarity of the interests and ideas of our children and adolescents, which make them different from the children and adolescents of Tsarist Russia and contemporary capitalist countries.

Education directs the psychological development of the child. It arises in the purposes set by our society and the policy of our state. The purpose of education includes a program of characteristics that the new generation should possess. These characteristics "must be expressed in the real traits of men who are formed by our pedagogical hands," as Makarenko put it. But even the purposes of education that the adults set for themselves also influence the psychological development of children, for they become to some extent the purposes and motives of the children's activities and determine the vitally important tasks which the children will be called upon to perform. Any educative task set before the child becomes an inner spur for his activity if the child takes it over to some extent and makes it *his own* task; as a result, the consciousness that it must be achieved creates in him the will to achieve it and to achieve it well. The higher the level of consciousness and self-knowledge in the child, the greater is the influence of the actual situation on the efficacy of his activities and the further is his development.

At later stages, the growing personality of the child, inspired by the opinions, beliefs, perspectives and ideals acquired through education, begins to direct the process of his own development, to correct personal defects, and to foster the growth of positive moral qualities.

It is here that a very significant characteristic of the psychological development of the human personality, which is particularly important for this process, makes itself felt. It is spontaneity. The art of educational guidance consists in arousing this spontaneity, in providing it with its required content, and in leading it in the right direction. It is the educators who know how to turn their children and pupils into their own conscious and active coeducators who achieve pedagogic work of high quality.

The driving forces of psychological development are to be sought neither in heredity or environment, nor in any combination of these "two factors," as is asserted by bourgeois psychological theories. They are rather contained in the life of the child himself. The development of the psyche as a special way of expressing life is characterized by the contradictions that belong to life and are specific to it.

These contradictions are not confined to those that develop in the course of physiological development. They are formed in the social conditions of the child's existence and find their solution in them, by making way for new contradictions.

A general characteristic of these contradictions is that they are contained in the tension arising between the level of psychological development already reached and the new problems set by life. The growing personality, under the influence of society and education, sets about solving these problems. The contradictions have a specific character at each stage of development. Thus, education at school, by placing the pupil before ever new and more difficult problems, inevitably creates contradictions between these problems and the existing level of development, motivation, ability and other psychological characteristics. The mastery of the fundamentals of science requires not only the utilization of existing possibilities but also the acquisition of entirely new knowledge, feelings and qualities of will.

The psychological development is thus explained as the overcoming of contradictions; the raising of psychological processes and characteristics to the level required to solve new vital tasks; the weeding out of old and the creation of new traits of consciousness and self-knowledge of personality; and, finally, as a constantly growing enrichment of psychological life. As in every other genuine development, some old traits disappear, while others, new ones, are formed, consolidated and developed. Thus, with advancing age, the direct and naive interests of the preschool child fade away and make place for the new, deeper, more serious and more constant interests of the school child. The purely childish ways of thinking disappear; they are replaced by newer and more developed ones, which correspond to the higher stage of knowledge of the surrounding world. Naturally, not everything fades away, much remains as solid attainment of personality. But even what remains is much transformed. Both in the history of the individual and of mankind, what grows cannot be defeated because it bears within itself the germs of the future. No education, even if it should set itself this absurd purpose, can, e.g., return the pupil to his childish interest in play and to his childish view of the world, of other men and of himself. He has already lived through them, and his entire being is directed towards the future.

The psychological development of the child consists of a sequence of regular and necessary stages. Each preceding stage prepares the following one and inevitably makes room for it. The actual possibilities of transition to a new stage are always created in the concrete life and activities of the child. Thus, the play and other activities of the preschool child, directed by education, create the possibilities for education at school and prepare for the systematic acquisition of knowledge there. These new opportunities do not grow by themselves; they come into being under certain definite social conditions, with the aid of the means provided by society, and under the decisive influence of education. Instruction and education of the child create new possibilities by realizing the existing ones, but in a different way and depending on the content and the methods by which the realization takes place.

This also applies to those potentialities of the child that we call his natural gifts. They are not only utilized in instruction and education; they undergo changes during the process. It is wrong to assume that the gifts of the child do not change, while his various abilities develop. But this wrong metaphysical conception of gifts is commonly accepted in bourgeois psychology.

Various bourgeois psychologists, like W. Stern, Binet, Claparède, Spearman, etc., use it as the starting point for working out systems of tests for the determination of "intelligence quotients," "natural doses of intelligence," "reserves of mental energy," etc. We find in our own scientific literature and practice remnants of this conception of natural gifts. They must be definitely overcome, so that the educators can successfully direct the development of the child's abilities.

Natural gifts are not ready abilities but only natural possibilities for the formation and development of such abilities. The material foundation of these possibilities is provided by the child's organism, and particularly by his brain, his senses and his organs of motion. These possibilities are, like the organism itself, a product of a development whose inner structure is different at different stages.

The child is born with a relatively highly developed nervous system, with senses and organs of motion, as well as with organic needs that stimulate him into activity. The degree of their development also determines the degree of development of his inborn gifts. Marx and Engels say that "the child is supplied by nature in part with natural forces, with life forces; it is an active, natural creature; these forces exist in him in the form of gifts, abilities and also of instincts. . . ."[14]

The growing interaction of the child and the world around him produces, by bringing out ever new psychological characteristics, a change in their anatomical and physiological foundations. Through this interaction, the child's organism develops; his nervous system matures, and especially his cerebral cortex; his functional characteristics grow; and a great mass of conditioned reflexes and other neurodynamic links are formed. The results of investigations by I. P. Pavlov and his disciples show that these connections and relations do not grow by themselves. They are formed in the child's activity, by the solution of all kinds of tasks set by life.

Therefore, the successes of the child in his psychological development presuppose the development of his natural abilities. The abilities, as the starting points for the psychological development, themselves grow while that development is taking place. For what does not itself develop, cannot be the inner condition of a development. The abilities of the child who starts going to school are no longer the same as those he had at the age of three, or when he was born, because the child himself is no longer the same. The abilities are always contained in their realization and in their concrete results. To every stage of development of the child's psyche there corresponds a stage in the development of his abilities. We cannot view this, of course, as an interaction of two factors which are parallel and of equal importance, for the psychological and physiological developments are not identical and their relationship is complex. On the other hand, psychological development must not be separated from the development of the material substratum and its potentialities.

To understand natural gifts correctly, it is necessary to abandon once and for all the conception that views them as powers which are localized in individual parts of the brain and which directly condition the development of individual abilities. Such a conception is not in keeping with the results of scientific studies of the work of the brain as the material substratum of psychological activity. Every concrete form of such activity, like reading, the solution of arithmetical problems, learning by heart, playing a piece of music, technical construction, is the expression of an *indivisible* human personality. The brain participates in these processes *as a whole,* even if its individual parts and structures are responsible for the different aspects of these complicated processes. Therefore, the natural gifts of the child develop *as a whole* in each of his activities, but they develop in different degrees and in different directions, according to the character of each activity and according

96

to the demands it makes on the child's personality.

We can estimate the natural abilities only to the extent in which a growing personality, all other conditions being equal, manifests itself in this or that kind of human activity and results in relevant skills or other qualities. A personality can manifest itself in many kinds of activities with equal success; it is thus that the general character of the natural gifts expresses itself. But, at the same time, the different branches of human activity—musical, technical, scientific, etc.—make specific demands on the human personality. The existence of special natural gifts for the development of individual abilities manifests itself in the way in which these demands are met.

It is understandable that the manifold and many-sided activity of the child in the family, in the kindergarten, at school and outside school is the decisive precondition for the development of natural gifts and talents. Whatever natural gifts for the development of general and special abilities the child might possess, they cannot be transformed by themselves, and apart from the corresponding activity, into scientific, musical, technical and other abilities. But this does not mean, of course, that natural gifts which are not utilized because of given conditions of life and activity are therefore dulled and finally die away, as is assumed by some people.

Such an opinion is derived from a false conception of natural gifts. It views them as some kind of isolated "organ" in the brain which dies away if it lies fallow. Actually, everything in the brain is activity; not only nothing dies, but everything develops further. The development of general abilities is also expressed in the special gifts, even if these are not utilized. A person can

97

be robbed, no doubt, by the conditions of his life, of the opportunity to learn, to acquire a mastery of the arts, and to enjoy them. But this does not mean that his natural gifts perish. They can make their appearance at a ripe old age. After the October Revolution, many workers who learned to read and write only at an advanced age, successfully acquired a knowledge of the achievements of science, technology and the arts. There is, for example, the case of E. I. Guseva. Born in a village of Simbirsk province, she learned to read and write when she was over forty. She became a student at a Workers' Faculty, graduated together with her son from the Timiryazev Agricultural Academy, obtained in 1936 the degree of the "Candidate of Sciences." Now, at the age of seventy-three, she has successfully defended a dissertation on the cultivation of some agricultural plants (Agrumen) and does creative work in agricultural technology. The name of E. I. Guseva, who trained hundreds of young specialists, is known in all collective and government farms of the Black Sea Coast. Her life story is typical of our country.

The gifts and abilities develop through purposeful activity, both in the child and in the adult. As Gorki put it: "The higher a man's purpose, the more rapidly and more productively his abilities and talents develop." Makarenko proved by his practical work the great importance of ideological purposefulness in the education and development of the growing personality. He stressed especially the value of men's more distant purposes, especially those which are linked with the aims and tasks of our society (cf. his "system of perspectives"). "Anticipated joy," he wrote, "is a true stimulus of human life." Therefore, "to educate a man" means to supply

98

him with perspectives to which an anticipation of joy is attached, beginning with the simplest kind of joy and ending with those which express the consciousness of the citizen of our country and his sentiment of duty to our society.

Without new purposes and perspectives linked with those of the collective, there would be no development and no progress.

Two abilities of educators play a very important part in the guidance of psychological development. One is the ability to transform these future perspectives into concrete tasks which must be achieved at a given stage of life and activity. The other is the capacity of arousing a conscious and interested attitude towards these tasks and of mobilizing all efforts for the overcoming of obstacles and difficulties. Both in the historical development of mankind and in the growth of the individual, work creates ever new possibilities for solving new problems. These result from overcoming the difficulties which arise in the child's learning and other activities. The acquisition of knowledge does not proceed without obstacles to be overcome as a precondition of the child's growth and mental development. It is only by overcoming difficulties that the child acquires a solid knowledge, forms his abilities and talents, develops his power of acquiring knowledge and other qualities, and forges his character. The intellectual maturity to which our schools certify their graduates is a result of ten years of systematic and strenuous work directed by educators.

One necessary precondition for the development of the potentialities of every child consists in the high demands made by the educator who must, however, adapt them to the child's strength and combine them with care, attention and respect for the child's personality. "Without demands there can be no education," Makarenko correctly noted. He remarked in this connection that in our country completely new demands were made both on adults and on growing personalities. But these demands, to be fulfilled, create new possibilities and new qualities of reason, emotion and will. The demands we make on growing personalities are the expression of our strong belief in their strength and their potentialities—they are, indeed, a necessary precondition for the realization of their abilities. They are in no contradiction with man; on the contrary, man recognizes their justice and turns them into demands upon himself, upon his own work and upon his qualities that are in the state of formation.

Ushinsky observed that the art of guiding the psychological development of personality is the most complicated and difficult of all arts. It consists in the ability to direct the life and activity of men. This work raises the educator to the level of an "engineer of the childish soul"; he creates new qualities in the child. And yet, he has one task that is even more difficult: to re-educate some children and to correct the mistakes of earlier educational work.

The success of the educator's task depends in the first place on his Communist purposefulness, his love for his work and his ability to use for his purpose all the rich means that our socialist society places at his disposal. But to do this he needs to know the children, their life, their nature, and their development. Engels' view that man rules nature only when he understands her laws applies both to the laws of outer nature and

100

to those laws to which the bodily and mental nature of man is subjected.

A true "engineer" of the child's consciousness is the educator who knows the laws of the human nature upon which he exercises an influence and which he helps to form; who knows the age and individual peculiarities of the child; who takes into account the concrete possibilities of each stage of development and creates new ones; who understands how to notice, behind seemingly insignificant facts, the germs of new qualities in the consciousness and self-consciousness of the child; who can help the child to develop these qualities and to use them for his growth. The realization that the psychological development of our children and the formation of their psychological and moral qualities takes place under the decisive influence of Communist education, confirms the powerful importance of the scientific study of the problems of child and educational psychology.

Notes

1. V. I. Lenin, from the *Posthumous Philosophical Writings* (in German), Berlin, Dietz, 1949, p. 190.

2. W. Preyer, *The Soul of the Child* (in German), 8th edition, Leipzig, 1912, pp. VI-VIII.

3. K. A. Timiryazev, *Works* (in Russian), 1939, vol. VI, p. 265.

4. *Ibid.*, pp. 183, 265.

5. K. Bühler, *The Mental Development of the Child* (in German), 6th edition, Jena, 1930, p. 39.

6. E. Huguenin, *The Children's Courts* (in French), Paris, 1935, p. 89.

7. E. L. Thorndike, *Man and His Works*, 1943, pp. 9, 12, 13, 15-16, 21, 40.

8. A. A. Zhdanov, "Contribution to the Philosophical Discussion" (in Russian), in *Voprosy Filozofii*, 1947, Nr. 1, p. 263.

9. Georges Politzer, *The Crisis of Contemporary Psychology* (in French), Paris, 1947, pp. 117, 119.

10. *Ibid.*, pp. 89, 91, 96, 109.

11. *Ibid.*, pp. 90, 117.

12. K. Marx and F. Engels, *Works,* IV (in Russian), p. 65.

13. V. I. Lenin, *Posthumous Philosophical Writings* (in German), Berlin, Dietz, p. 31.

14. K. Marx and F. Engels, *Works* (in Russian), vol. III, p. 642.

INVESTIGATION OF
PUPIL PERSONALITY

A. L. Shnirman

The foundations for the psychological study of personality and the possibilities of such an investigation have been established by one of the most important theses of Soviet psychology: man's consciousness and the psychological qualities of his personality are formed and express themselves in activity. This assertion is of fundamental importance. The thesis that psychological characteristics are formed through activity opens wide perspectives for the development of necessary human qualities through the correct guidance of human experience. The fact that man's consciousness and psychological characteristics are prominent in any purposeful activity, offers us a possibility for an all-round understanding of human personality.

Idealist psychology decries the possibility of understanding the psyche of another person through his behavior. On this basis, self-observation or introspection developed as the only method of psychological investigation. "Objective" psychology directed upon behavior, i.e., behaviorism, which is a variety of idealistic psychology, also denied that it was possible to understand scientifically a man's psyche from its manifestations. This conception led to the conclusion that psychology must renounce altogether an understanding of the psyche and must study only the outward behavior of man in connection with the environment that influences him, as a totality of reactions and reflexes. Thus, all the tendencies of bourgeois psychology agree that man's psyche cannot be understood.

Soviet psychology, based on logical Marxist theory, consistently asserts the thesis of the understandability of the psyche. The possibility of a scientific understanding of the psyche is derived from the recognition that the psyche, formed in human activity, manifests itself in human activity.

The above account yields our first principle for the study of human personality generally and of pupil personality in particular, i.e., the study of personality in its activity. To give this study a real content, we must analyse personality from many sides through its different forms of activity.

The most essential and important activity of the pupil is learning. We must therefore study the personality of the pupil in the learning process. The teacher notices many psychological traits of his pupils in the course of his instruction in class. It is the interests of the pupil that manifest themselves here: his likings for this or that subject, the extension and depth of his interests, his constancy and his activity, the peculiarity of his behavior. The pupil's behavior in class expresses important motivations of his actions, and, above all, his personal convictions. These manifest themselves in his attitude towards schoolwork (conscientiousness and a sense of responsibility in work) ; his position as regards ideological questions, especially in literature, history, biology and physics; his high opinion of this or that historical character, personality of public life, an outstanding artist, scientist or writer—any man for whom he has a special sympathy and who becomes his ideal. We also obtain information about the pupil's motivations in learning, when we analyse his reactions to the teacher's judgments on his work and behavior. What is interesting here is the type of the pupil's reaction. The following reactions are typical: a correct attitude in estimating his grades, viewed both as a just estimate of his work and as a stimulus to further efforts; an indifferent attitude; over-estimation of the value of grades and constant effort to get ones; differential attitude to good or bad grades and their varied effect on the pupil's activity; etc. Very important also is the pupil's attitude to the judgment of different teachers, according to the nature of the subject, the personal qualities of the teacher and the pupil's relationship with him.

The abilities of the pupil in this or that area of studies manifest themselves in class with a particular clarity. A sufficient degree of attention permits the teacher to recognize not only the actual state of the pupil's abilities, but also the direction of their development. The teacher observes in class many essential facts which help him to understand the pupil's traits and habits, especially the qualities of his schoolwork, e.g., correctness, eagerness and grade.

The intellectual characteristics of the pupil manifest themselves with special distinctness: gift of observation; rapid grasp; careful understanding; clear, distinct and graphic language; logical thought; expression that goes straight to the point; clear and vivid speech, and other traits that impressively characterize the pupil's mentality. The same is true of the characteristics of the pupil's will: activity; perseverance; persistence; the capacity to overcome difficulties; initiative; independence; self-control; etc.

It is more difficult to recognize the pupil's emotional characteristics from his behavior in class. But this side, too, of the pupil's personality will manifest itself to a greater or lesser degree. The teacher who observes his pupil closely can always recognize the different expressions of "intellectual" feelings: thirst for knowledge; joy in the successful accomplishment of a difficult task, etc. But he can also note the existence of aesthetic feeling, e.g., in the literature class; and of moral feelings which manifest themselves with special clarity in the treatment of ideological questions.

The teacher has many opportunities in class to observe manners of the pupil's behavior that are characteristic of his attitude towards other people. They show themselves in the pupil's relationship with the teacher, in his reactions to the teacher's instructions and his stimulating or reproving remarks. Very important for the characterization of a pupil are his relations with his fellow pupils, e.g., gruff or cooperative behavior; rudeness or politeness; sensitivity; envy; arrogance or condescension, etc. Typical of the pupil's behavior is his attitude towards the achievements of the other pupils in class, to their progress or failure.

Another type of characteristics of the pupil that manifest themselves in class includes those which indicate his feelings about himself: modesty or presumption; self-confidence or timidity; ambition, etc.

106

Thus even a simple observation in class reveals to the teacher a series of important character traits of the pupil. But a true teacher does not limit himself to a passive observation of the pupil. He deliberately creates conditions in which certain character traits of the pupil, which are of interest to him, manifest themselves. He gives serious thought to the demands to be made on that particular pupil, to the manner of their presentation, to whether praise or censure is appropriate, to the effect that a special interest in the pupil's personal development or indifference towards him might have. These observations of the teacher in class are supplemented by the results of his control of the pupil's achievements, his classwork and homework, his notes, statements and summaries, his themes and his essays, especially those on "free" themes, e.g. on friendship and comradeship; on ideals and plans for the future, etc. These observations and reflections offer the teacher a rich material for characterizing the growing personalities of his pupils.

But the teacher must not limit himself to what he notes at school. Many character traits of the pupil manifest themselves more clearly and significantly in other forms of his activity. Above all, the extra-curricular activities of the pupil offer the teacher great opportunities for studying his personality. These activities include work in various groups; his contributions to wall newspapers and pupils' magazines; his participation in readers' circles, sport clubs, etc. The mere fact that these activities are usually carried out without compulsion and on the pupil's own initiative makes them particularly valuable in revealing his motives—and interests. Breadth, depth and constancy of these interests show themselves with special clarity in extra-curricular activities. The literary interests of the pupil merit a special attention. Unfortunately, they very often remain outside the teacher's field of awareness, though they are of great importance for a study of the personality of young people.

Also to be noted is the pupil's interest in questions of Soviet and international politics. The pupil's tendencies in this respect show themselves in classes on political information, in political lectures and in judgments of newspaper items.

Very important is the study of the pupil's conduct in social situations. Many important traits of character, especially the pupil's attitude towards his school and his class, manifest themselves here. Thus it becomes clear how the successes and failures of his class affect him. His sense of responsibility towards the collective and his consciousness of the responsibility of his class collective towards the school show themselves particularly in the performance of common tasks and especially of the tasks assigned to him by the class and to the class by the school. Many personality traits manifest themselves in social situations and in relations with the collective. They include: communicativeness; sympathy; attention; openness; love of truth; sincerity; confidence; friendliness, etc. It is in the collective that an understanding of collective life is formed and developed, and also the ability to fit in and to subordinate oneself, which are important characteristics of the will. It is in the collective that the social feelings of men form and manifest themselves.

The study of the pupil at his social work and in his collective are therefore an important part of the teacher's analysis of pupil personality.

Learning in class, extra-curricular activities, and social work are the most important spheres of the pupil's activities. They offer the teacher the best clues to the pupil's psychological traits. But it would be wrong for the teacher to ignore another very important part of the pupil's life, i.e., his activity at home and with his family. We don't mean the pupil's homework, but rather his mutual relations with the family, the chores assigned to him and his collaboration in the functioning of the home. It may happen that the pupil learns well in class and takes an active part in the school collective, but he won't do a stroke of work at home and insists that the family do everything for him. The school and the teacher must not ignore such facts.